Do-It-Yourself
Debt Repair

by Jay Butler and
Dr. Robert Hagopian
AssetProtectionServices.com

ISBN 978-0-9914644-7-0

DO-IT-YOURSELF **DEBT REPAIR**

TAKE CONTROL OF YOUR FINANCIAL FUTURE

Table of **Contents**

Section 4   United States Code (USC), Title 15, Chapter 41, SubChapter V, § 1692 (a-p) Fair Debt Collection Practices Act (FDCPA) § 801-818

Disclaimer

The publication is copyrighted © 2016 by Asset Protection Services of America (hereinafter "APSA") with all rights reserved. No part of this publication may be reproduced, retransmitted or rebroadcast in any form or by any means without the express prior written consent of the copyright holder.

Information contained in this publication has been prepared for continuing research and, although these materials may be technical in nature, carries no weight other than being educational in purpose. The materials are provided only as a starting point in order for the reader to undertake his or her own investigation of the subject matter contained herein.

This publication has been garnered from sources deemed reliable at the time of rendering. Since laws, rules, rulings, regulations, statutes and codes are constantly changing and evolving, the information may not be current and APSA takes no responsibility for updating, omitting or correcting any information in this publication.

APSA offers no guarantees the information in this book as being comprehensive, exhaustive, accurate or complete and furthers the information provided is on an "AS IS" basis. Any guidance or reliance on the content found in this publication is at the sole risk of the user. APSA offers no assurances as to the suitability of any particular service or strategy meeting any stated aims, goals or objectives. APSA strongly recommends the reader seek independent accounting, financial, investing, legal, tax or other professional advice.

No representations or warranties are given or implied to render any accounting, financial, investing, legal, tax or other professional advice. No accounting, financial, investing, legal, tax or other professional advice is intended, approved or authorized by APSA. If any accounting, financial, investing, legal, tax or other professional advice is required, then a competent professional should be sought.

APSA and any APSA advisors, directors, employees, members, officers, partners, professional agencies, professional intermediaries, shareholders, staff, ultimate beneficial owners and any other affiliated firms or third-parties wherever situated, take no responsibility whatsoever, whether individually or collectively, for the manner in which the reader may choose to interpret or use the information presented in this publication. APSA shall not be held liable for any civil or criminal liability or damages whether direct, indirect, special or consequential resulting from any interpretations or use of the information provided in this publication.

This publication shall not be taken as sanctioning or advocating any unlawful act or for any improper use of any entity structure, asset protection, tax strategy or estate planning activity, nor for any illegal or fraudulent purposes.

Asset Protection Services of America

The inverted "V" displayed on our shield is the uppercase letter "L" in ancient Greek identifying the people of Lacedaemonia, which in historical times was the proper name for the Spartan state. The Greek cry "Molôn Labé" means "Come and Get Them" as spoken by King Leonidas in response to the Persian army's demand for the outnumbered Spartans (300 against 300,000) to surrender their weapons during battle in the narrow pass or 'hot gates' of Thermopylae in 480 B.C. The iconic expression has become a symbol of courage to defend that which belongs to you, even if faced against overwhelming or insurmountable odds.

Author

Jay Butler is the Managing Director of Asset Protection Services of America, the former Managing Director of Asset Protection Services International, Ltd and the former Vice-President of Sales and Marketing for Corporate Support Services of Nevada Inc. Mr. Butler holds a Bachelor's Degree of Fine Arts from Boston University.

Jay has provided customized business entity structuring for clients in all 50 states along with some of the most respected names in the industry including the Jay Mitton organization "the father of asset protection" and Real Estate Investor Association seminars.

While working with Wealth Protection Concepts, LLC under the tutelage of the former Las Vegas and North Las Vegas city attorney Carl E. Lovell Jr. (now deceased from Leukemia), Mr. Butler was bestowed the title of "Asset Protection Planner" for his competency and experience. He also co-authored the first edition of his book "Cover Your Assets: Legal Authorities on Asset Protection, Tax Strategies and Estate Planning" © 2006 with Dr. Lovell.

While residing in Switzerland, Mr. Butler was the Associate Director of "CO-Handelszentrum GmbH" providing Swiss company formation and administration services and executed a full-range of fiduciary responsibilities including sales, client support and international corporate compliance services (KYC, FATCA, AML, FATF and Swiss Code of Obligations).

Jay builds his relationships through consistent attention to detail and reliable support. He has traveled extensively throughout the United States (having visited 49 of the 50 states), explored 36 nations worldwide, and has lived in a total of 7 countries throughout North America, Central America, the Middle East, North Africa and Europe.

Dr Robert Hagopian is semi-retired and the former CEO of Nevada Trustee Services Group Inc, which has provided trustee services to attorneys and law firms throughout the United States since 2005, and the former CEO of the Commerce Bank Ltd in Hong Kong.

Since 1968, Robert has traveled extensively throughout Asia and lived in Japan, Hong Kong and the Philippines with current residency and offices in Manilla.

Dr. Hagopian holds a Bachelor of Science (BS) degree in business administration, an MsD (doctorate) in philosophy and a "jure Dignitatis" Bachelor of Laws degree.

Since 1984, Dr. Hagopian has been structuring business entities for optimum wealth preservation, profitability, asset protection and limiting personal liability through the use of domestic corporations, limited liability companies and various trust vehicles.

Robert has developed innovative processes for the acquisition, holding and marketing of real property. In 2008, Dr. Hagopian applied for the patent-pending "Equity Recovery Program". Based on IRC 351 rules for the transference of real estate to a corporation, the program lawfully avoids capital gains tax, self-employment and state taxes upon the sale of real property.

Contact Us

Please browse our website at www.AssetProtectionServices.com and contact us to schedule your free private asset protection consultation. We welcome the opportunity to hold a 3-way conference call with your tax advisor and/or legal counsel to address any specific questions or concerns you may have. Experience has demonstrated it favorable to have all related parties "on the same page" when creating your structure.

Asset Protection Services of America
701 South Carson Street (Suite #200)
Carson City, Nevada 89701-5239
Office (775) 461-5255
Skype Jay_Butler
E-Mail info@AssetProtectionServices.com
Website www.AssetProtectionServices.com

Books by Jay Butler
and Dr. Robert Hagopian

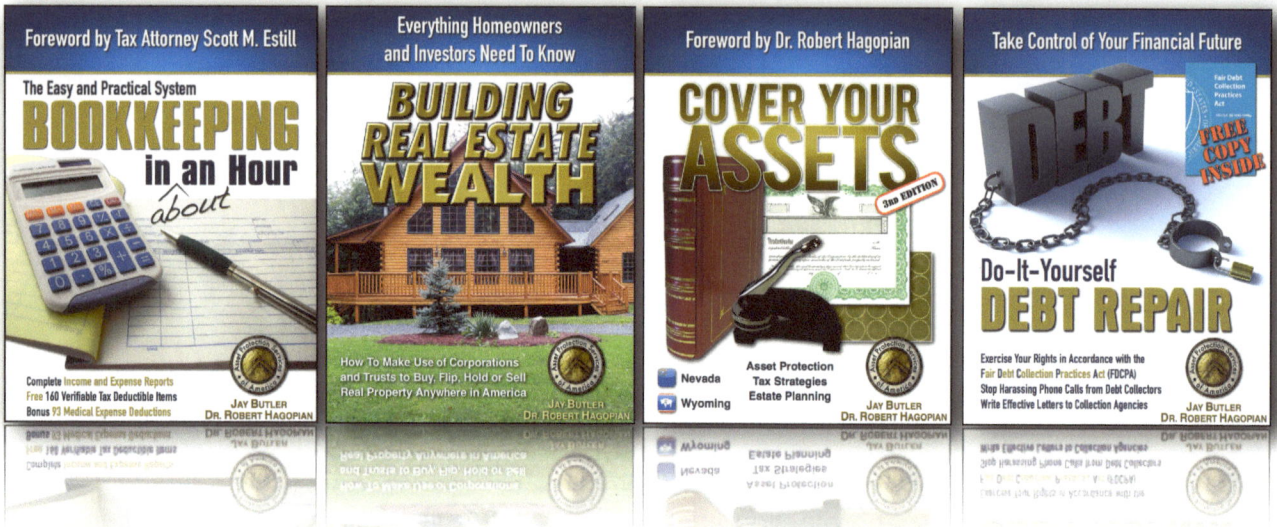

Foreword by Tax Attorney Scott M. Estill	Everything Homeowners and Investors Need To Know	Foreword by Dr. Robert Hagopian	Take Control of Your Financial Future

Bookkeeping in About an Hour — ISBN 978-0-9914644-0-1
Building Real Estate Wealth — ISBN 978-0-9914644-1-8
Cover Your Assets *(3rd Edition)* — ISBN 978-0-9914644-2-5
Do-It-Yourself Debt Repair — ISBN 978-0-9914644-7-0

Where to Apply for a Second Passport	Foreword by Attorney Glenn D. Godfrey	Thriving on 100% Straight Commission	So... How Do I Run My Company?

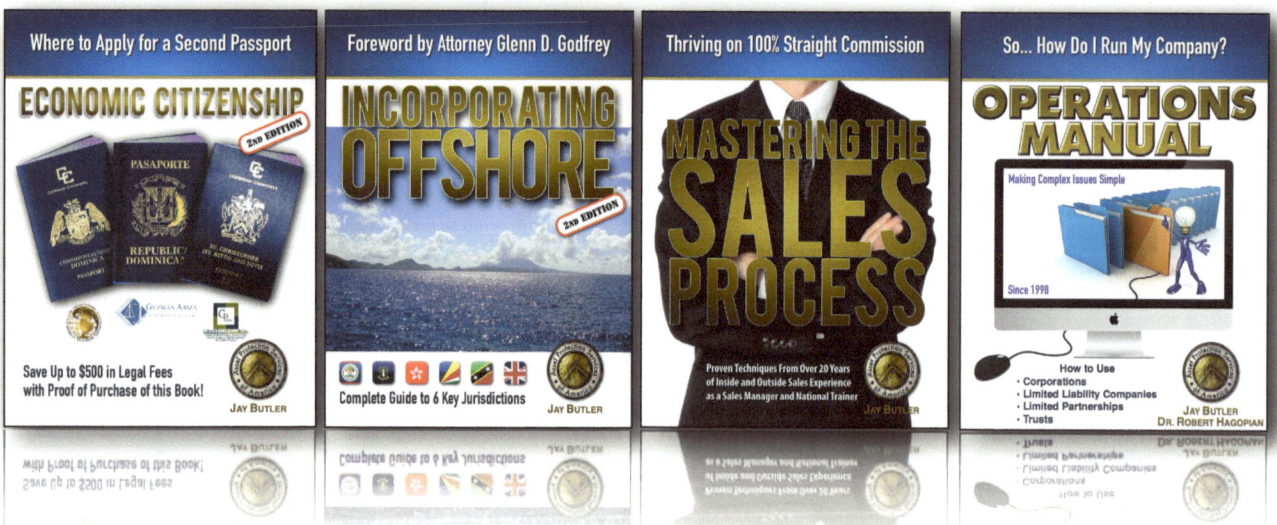

Economic Citizenship *(2nd Edition)* — ISBN 978-0-9914644-4-9
Incorporating Offshore *(2nd Edition)* — ISBN 978-0-9914644-5-6
Mastering the Sales Process — ISBN 978-0-9914644-6-3
Operations Manual — ISBN 978-0-9914644-3-2

Take Control of Your Financial Future

AssetProtectionServices.com

Dealing with Your Original Creditors

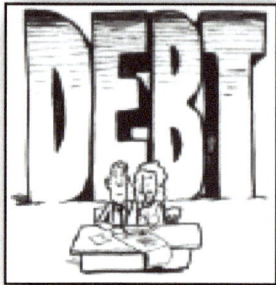

Your original creditor is the company from whom you originally obtained credit or otherwise borrowed money, and if your account is 90-120 days past due you are probably dealing with them. However, if your account is over 120 days in default, then you are probably dealing with a collection agency right now. The laws and rules are different for collection agencies than those for original creditor collectors.

First and foremost, if you know that you are not going to be able to pay your bills, contact your creditor right away. Most creditors will try and work out hardship terms with you for a certain period of time. (See our Forms) This may include a reduction in interest, waiving late fees or they may even not report the debt as past due with the credit-reporting agencies. We cannot stress enough that it is best to call them as soon as possible.

Useful Tips When Negotiating with Your Original Creditors

Always be polite no matter what happens. This will get you further than anything else when negotiating with a creditor. Creditors spend most of their time dealing with angry and difficult customers. Be courteous and the creditor will likely be more prone to give you what you want. Let the creditor know that you are willing to compromise. Creditors need to meet their objectives too. If you present a win-win situation, then the creditor can feel good about the negotiation. If your original creditors refuse to negotiate when you first contact them don't take it personally. Wait a few days or weeks and then try again.

Explain your situation, but don't over-explain it. Tell the creditor what you can do, rather than what you can't do. Don't ask the creditor how much they will accept, but tell the creditor how much you can pay. Remember not to offer to pay more than you can afford.

Start negotiating as soon as possible. Negotiating with the original creditor is much easier than dealing with a collection agency later. If you can't afford to pay all creditors at once, negotiate a settlement with the creditor with the smallest balance. Once that debt is paid in full, negotiate with the creditor with the next highest balance and so on.

Most creditors are willing to negotiate a settlement for less than the full amount of the debt. Some creditors will even accept as little as 40-70 percent of the debt, especially for unsecured credit card debts.

Get all settlement agreements in writing. Keep copies of all letters, e-mails, statements, phone call conversations and other communications for your files.

---

10 Steps to Negotiating a Debt Settlement

1 Gather all the documentation, amounts due, credit reports, penalties and interest for all of your debts. Then anticipate the total amount you can comfortably afford to settle or pay on a monthly basis.

2 Call each creditor and ask to speak with someone who has the authority to make settlement arrangements and change what they report to the credit-reporting agencies.

3 Unemotionally explain your situation to each creditor. Explain why you have not been able to make your payments and what your plans are for settling the debt you owe them.

4 When you make your offer, remember that if they sell the debt to a collection agency they will be making pennies on the dollar. Make an offer to settle the debt and ask that they report it "paid as agreed, closed by consumer". *Be prepared that the best you may be able to get is to have it reported as "settled" because many companies may refuse to report it "paid as agreed".* But if you don't ask, you surely won't get what reflects the best for you.

5 If they do not agree to your offer, politely thank them for their time and hang up. Try again in a few days. I have found that the phone reps are very black-and-white in that they are either rude and unwilling to help or they are very nice and helpful. If they are rude, wait and talk to someone else. If they refuse to negotiate at all, ask to speak with a supervisor. Explain what you are offering and be sure to ask for the agreement in writing. Make notes about with whom you spoke and what they agreed to do.

6 If you have no luck negotiating on the phone, send them a letter detailing the reasons why you are in default, a listing of the total debts you owe, a copy of your credit report showing that you are in default on more than just their account, your monthly budget showing that there is not enough income to make payments and your best offer to settle the debt.

7 Be sure to get the agreement in writing before you pay a penny. If you don't get it in writing you are trusting that they will do what they say. Most won't and you will have no legal recourse at that time, unless you have it in writing.

8 NEVER send post-dated checks. There have been far too many instances of creditors cashing those post-dated checks as soon as they receive them. The bank will pay them and you have no legal recourse as to the consequences.

9 Once you have the settlement amount, wait to get the settlement agreement in writing from the creditor. This letter will protect you from any future claims from that creditor. There have been instances where agreements have been reached, payment made and then the company comes back for the balance due at a later date. If you don't have it in

writing, you might as well expect to pay it. We have drafted a very good settlement agreement that is included in the forms section toward the end of this publication. Once you have the settlement letter in hand, pay the agreed upon amount by money order or cashier's check promptly as agreed.

10 Check your credit report at each of the credit-reporting agencies in about 60-90 days to verify that it has been updated as agreed. If not, send a copy of the agreement letter to the creditor AND the credit-reporting agencies and request (in writing) that your credit file be updated immediately per your agreement with the creditor.

You may owe taxes. Once you settle a credit card debt or settle other debts, creditors more than likely will have forgiven a percentage of what you owed them. This forgiven debt, known as "cancellation-of-debt", is taxable as income to you per IRS guidelines. Your creditor very well might send you a 1099 at the end of the year for the amount of money that was forgiven (the amount you didn't have to pay) and it may be subject to taxation by the IRS.

Collection Agencies

If you've been making late payments or you haven't paid for months, your creditors may send your debt (account) for "collections". That is, your creditor may pass on your account to its "in-house" collection department or hire a third-party collection agency to collect the debt from you. They may even "sell" your account to a third-party debt collector who may in turn "sell" the debt to yet another third-party debt collector.

Who are third-party debt collectors? Third-party debt collectors (also known as bill collectors) work for collection agencies and try all sorts of means to collect payments from you.

When your original creditor sends your account to its "in-house" collection department, it retains all original rights to your account because the "in-house" collector simply acts on behalf of the original creditor and not on behalf of any third-party.

However, when the original creditor "sells" your account to a third-party debt collector (also known as a collection agency), the third-party debt collector then becomes the "owner" of your account and the debt it represents. When your original creditor "sells" your account to a third-party it is called a "charge-off".

Generally when your account has been charged-off the new owner of the account very seldom has, nor can they acquire, a copy of the original contract which you signed. This is VERY IMPORTANT because without that document, you can stop them cold! This is especially true in foreclosures. In most cases the original mortgage that you signed has been sold and resold several times. And recent court cases have stopped the foreclosure process by creditors until the original contract signed by the debtor can be produced.

What Debt Collectors Cannot Do

The Fair Debt Collection Practices Act, which comes from the United States Code (USC), Title 15, Chapter 41, SubChapter V, § 1692 (a-p), *hereinafter referred to as the* **FDCPA**, regulates debt collectors who work for collection agencies as well as collection agencies themselves. However, the act does not apply to debt collectors that are employed by the original creditor (the business or person who first extended you credit or loaned you money). The FDCPA prohibits debt collectors from engaging in abusive behavior, including these 10 activities:

1 Calling you repeatedly or contacting you at an unreasonable time (the law presumes unreasonable to be before 8 a.m. or after 9 p.m.).

2 Place telephone calls to you without identifying themselves as bill collectors.

3 Contact you at work if your employer prohibits it.

4 Use obscene or profane language or threaten to use violence.

5 Claim you owe more than you do.

6 Claim to be attorneys if they are not.

7 Claim that you will be imprisoned or your property will be seized.

8 Send you anything that resembles a legal document, unless they are attorneys.

9 Add unauthorized interest, fees or charges.

10 Contact third-parties other than your attorney, a credit-reporting bureau or the original creditor, except for the limited purpose of finding information about where to find you. Unless you have asked collectors in writing to stop contacting you, they can also contact your spouse and your co-debtors.

How to Handle Debt Collectors and Stop Collection Calls

Here are some helpful tips on how to handle debt collectors and debt collection agencies.

Stop avoiding debt collectors. If you don't communicate with bill collectors, things may get worse and the collectors may even take you to court and get an order to garnish your wages.

Do not talk to debt collectors on the phone for any legnth of time. You need to have written proof of all negotiations and agreements that you make and telphone conversations are not binding on the collectors. All correspondence should be by Certified Mail with Return

Receipt. You will want proof to send to the Credit-Reporting Agencies and/or any Federal agencies should you file a lawsuit against the collection agency (which you may wish to do).

If you do end up speaking to a debt collector on the phone, you must take charge of the conversation immediately so that you are not "tricked" into making any admissions and confessions or, worse yet, agreeing to send them money. In order to take charge, there is a set of questions that we have drafted (next page) that will keep you on the right track.

Generally, when you start asking these questions the debt collector will want to get off the phone as quickly as possible. While you have a right to ask these questions, the debt collectors become intimidated when you ask for this information. Asking these questions to debt collectors and creditors can be quite enjoyable. Try it and you may find you like it!

Don't reveal too much information about your finances. Don't speak about your finances in detail because debt collectors are really only interested in collecting money from you. Remember that any information that you impart to the collector can be used against you.

Always keep records (or record) your conversations. Keep a record of the collectors you've spoken to, the time and summary of your conversation. You can use such records as proof against collectors and collection agencies who violate the law. You can even tape record the conversation (secret taping is allowed by approximately 35 states and the District of Columbia). However, if secret taping isn't allowed in your state, you will need to notify the collector that you will be taping the conversation before you begin taping.

Remember too, that in every case the collector will be taping every word you say. If he/she will not accept you taping him/her, then why in the world would you allow a collector to tape what you say? Think about it and become proactive. If they refuse to allow you to record the conversation, consider hanging-up and communicate with them via written letter.

How To Answer Creditor Telephone Calls
at Home

When you are contacted by a creditor and answer the telephone at home, ask the person calling to "hold" while you get a pen, paper and take a deep breathe to collect your thoughts.

When you return, be very polite and begin asking them the following questions. Be sure to write down their responses on paper and don't let them side-track you. Remember, you are in charge of the call. **Keep Control of Yourself and the Person Calling No Matter What!**

1   What is your full name please?
         - Please spell that for me slowly.
2   Which creditor specifically are you representing?
3   Are you a collection agency?
         - If yes, which one?
         - If not, whom specifically do you represent?
4   What is your complete mailing address please?
5   What is your direct telephone number and your extension please?

After you have received the answers to the above questions say, *"Thank you for calling"* and then ***Hang-up the Phone!!!***

If the creditor calls you back say, *"Thank you for calling"* and then ***Hang-up the Phone!!!***

How To Answer Creditor Telephone Calls
at Work

When you are contacted by a creditor and answer the telephone at work simply say, "My employer does not allow me to accept calls at work" and then ***Hang-up the Phone!!***

What You Should NEVER Do

NEVER answer any of the caller's questions. Always stick to the script above. Even if they ask you a question, ask them a question right back! Remember that your creditors are calling you to get information and money from you. They are not interested in being your friend!

NEVER discuss any financial arrangements or make payment plans over the phone with your creditors. All arrangement must be set out in writing only, never over the phone.

NEVER return any creditor calls. Once you have obtained answers to the above questions, all further communications shall be made in writing via Certified Mail with Return Receipt.

Debt Validation

Are you sure collection agencies are legally entitled to collect the debt they claim you owe? Before you make any payments to them, it is imperative that you find out if the collection agency has the right to collect the debt from you at all. This is where debt validation is one of the most important moves you can undertake.

The Federal Trade Commission (FTC) and the Fair Debt Collections Practices Act (FDCPA) requires that a collection agency send you a written notice of the amount of the debt, who the original creditor was as well as a notice that if you dispute the debt in writing they must provide you with written *validation* of the debt.

When you dispute the debt in writing, the collection agency must cease and desist trying to collect the debt until they provide you with written validation of the debt. *Validation can only be in the form of the original-signed contract between you and the original creditor!*

In addition to not being allowed to continue trying to collect the debt, they are also not allowed to report the debt to a credit-reporting agency or to sue you for the debt during this period. Any of these actions would place the collection agency in violation of the Federal Debt Collection Practices Act (FDCPA).

If bill collectors continue to contact you after receiving a cease and desist letter from you, you need only remind them that they are violating the FDCPA and that you will file a complaint with the FTC (Federal Trade Commission) at https://www.ftccomplaintassistant.gov and/or your State Attorney General. Even the U.S. Post Service will many times assist you with this because the collector used the U.S. Postal Services and thus violated the law by sending you collection letters after you sent them a "Notice of Cease and Desist".

Debt Validation Information

Original Creditors The FDCPA gives you the right to seek validation from a collection agency but not from an original creditor. This is because the FDCPA in no way governs the collection practices of original creditors, only the practices of third-party collection agencies.

Statute of Limitations You need to know if the creditor (or the collection agency) can seek money from you legally. Every state has a statute of limitations, which means that after a certain period of time has expired you are no longer liable for a debt. However, be aware that this stature of limitations runs from the date you made your last payment and not from the date of the original debt.

Debt Validation Debt validation is wherein you find out whether the collection agency actually has the legal right to ask you for money or even to discuss your debt with you. It is a process wherein you request the collection agency prove you legally owe their agency money. You entered into a contract with the original creditor, but **not** with the collection agency!

Proof of Validation If the collection agency is able to provide proof of validation in its original signed format, *which is exceedingly rare,* your next step is to begin negotiating a settlement with them in writing by Certified Mail with Return Receipt. Remember that the original creditor has written this debt off (charge-off) and sold it for pennies on the dollar to the collection agency. Therefore, you should start your offers as low as 30% of the original debt amount. If you can pay your offer immediately upon reaching agreement you stand a better chance of settling for a very low amount. If not, you should request a reasonable repayment schedule.

Time Limits for Debt Validation Under the FDCPA, collection agencies are required to send you a debt validation notice within 30 days of contacting you for the collection of a debt. The notice informs you of your right to validate / dispute the debt within 30 days. In cases where you don't dispute the debt (or request its validation) within the 30-day period, the collection agency has the legal right to assume that your debt is valid and may continue to try and collect the debt from you.

30-Day Debt Validation If a collection agency does not validate a debt within 30-days you need to send the collection agency a written request by Certified Mail with Return Receipt requesting they remove any negative listing which they may have sent to credit-reporting agencies. Include in that correspondence a copy of the original request for the debt validation and a copy of the return receipt. You should also contact each credit-reporting agency, which shows a negative entry from the collection agency by sending them a letter (in the same manner) with copies of the information described above. Validating the debt will be your most important ally in thwarting any collection agency attempts to collect money from you.

Debt Verification vs. Debt Validation

Debt Verification is a way in which many collection agencies try to side-step the issue of validating a debt. In the "validation" of debt the collector is required to send copies of the original contract you signed with the original creditor. But in a debt "verification", the collector need only provide a written statement showing the name and address of the original creditor and the total debt amount. **Verfifcation of debt is NOT a Validation of debt!**

Remember, you require *Validation* not verification. Stick to your guns, because unless there have been some dramatic changes recently, most collection agencies will be unable to acquire a copy of your original signed contract. "Too bad, so sad" for the collection agency!
When you request a validation of debt from a collection agency, they must provide you with all of the following specific details, if you request it in writing.

Disputing Debts after the Validation Period has Past You can send in a validation letter request to your collection agency after the 30-day period, but the collection agency is not legally obligated to give you a reply. They may also not stop collections on the account. So, trying to dispute debt after the validation period is over is not recommended.

When Debts are Assigned to a Collection Agency If your debt has been assigned to a collection agency, it implies that the collection agency legally doesn't own the debt. So, you cannot owe them money because it is a debt obligation between you and the original creditor only. However having stated the obvious, you may have signed the original contract stating that you'll be responsible for payments to the creditor **and/or its assigns**. Should this clause be in the contract you signed with your original creditor the contract actually is a contract between you, the creditor and any and all future collection agencies (i.e. collectors). Thus, if the collection agency provides you with a copy of a signed contract containing a clause like this then, sadly, you'll have to acknowledge and pay the debt to the collection agency.

Proof the Collection Agency Owns Your Debt You will need to request written proof that your debt has been sold or assigned to a collection agency. The contract between your original creditor and the collection agency would be their best proof of this fact, however they are highly unlikely to provide such documentation. And even if they are able to provide this documentation, it does not always prove that you are a party to their newly created contract.

Your Payment History You can request a "statement of account" detailing your payment history to date. This will help you to verify the total debt the of the original creditor verses the amount (including any added late fees / extra fees) that the collection agency has calculated and is attempting to charge.

State License Number You should also request for proof that the collection agency is licensed to collect debts in your state. Not all states impose licensing requirements for collection agencies including California, Georgia, Iowa, Kansas, Kentucky, Montana, Oklahoma, Pennsylvania and South Carolina. But if a collector needs a license to collect debts in your state, and the collection agency contacting you is not licensed in your state, send the them a letter stating how they've violated your state collection laws. You may also inform them that they may be subject to prosecution from your state and have to pay fines if they continue trying to collect money from you.

Copy of Your Original Signed Contract This is the single most important document! This will prove whether or not you still owe the debt and if the collection agency has any right to be contacting you at all. Watch out because instead of providing the original contract, collection agencies often try to provide "account statements" or other types of instruments from the original creditor. Should they opt for this statement, which they misleadingly call a "**Verification** of Debt", repudiate it immediately and again demand a "**Validation** of Debt" as evidenced by a copy of the original contract with the original creditor showing your signature.

Remind them that, by law, this is the ***only way*** you can be assured this debt is a debt owed by you!

What Happens if the Collection Agency is Unable to Validate the Debt?

If the collection agency doesn't send you satisfactory proof of the debt and the items you requested in your validation letter, then according to the FDCRA, the collection agency cannot collect any money from you nor can they legally contact you again!

Remove Collection Listing Under the FDCRA, collection agencies should not report a negative entry to the credit-reporting agencies if they don't validate your debt. You should send the collection agency a letter demanding that they remove any negative listing if they have already listed any. You should also inform them that if they don't remove any collection listing that they might have reported, you might sue them for violating your rights under the FDCPA. Wait 15-20 days for a reply from the collection agency. They'll either remove any negative listing or else they won't respond at all.

You Can Sue a Collector if an Inaccurate Listing is Not Removed If a collection agency doesn't remove an inaccurate collection listing from the report, then you can file a lawsuit in your local small claims court for their flagrant violation of the FDCPA and report them to the FTC under the FDCPA. However, prior to filing the lawsuit, inform the credit-reporting agencies that the collection agency has not removed the negative collection information from your credit report and ask them to do so.

Dealing with Credit-Reporting Agencies

If the credit-reporting agencies verify a collection activity you'll have proof of further collection activity on the part of the errant collection agency which, without a proven debt validation, is a violation of the FDCPA. You need to send proof of this violation to the credit-reporting agencies. You should request the method of validation of your collection listing (as allowed by the FDCPA). In case the credit-reporting agencies do not share the details of such validation, remind them that they are violating the FDCRA as well.

You can file a lawsuit against an errant credit-reporting agency on the basis that they couldn't provide you with a satisfactory method of validation. This can be done through the small claims court or your state. Just inform the errant credit-reporting agency about your intention to file a lawsuit, as there's a good chance that they will contact the collection agency to find out if the debt is legitimate. In such case, the credit-reporting agency will likely delete the collection listing right away.

Do You Need Additional Help?

If you believe you are a victim of unfair or illegal debt collection tactics, then submit your information to "Fair Debt Lawyer" for **FREE** at Fair-Debt-Collection.com or visit:

http://www.fair-debt-collection.com/ask-questions-form.html
Search by State for **FREE** assistance at:
http://www.fair-debt-collection.com/lawyer-locator.html
or Call Toll-Free at: 1-888-FDCPA-LAW

The Fair Debt Collection Practices Act prohibits abusive practices by debt collectors as amended by Public Law 104-208, 110 Stat. 3009 (Sept. 30, 1996). Debt collectors may be liable to you for statutory damages of up to $1,000 plus damages suffered and attorney fees! as described here: http://www.fair-debt-collection.com/fair-debt-act.html

Attorney General Complaint Forms for Filing Complaints Against Debt Collectors who Violate FDCPA and State Debt Collection Laws

The state links below are to the consumer complaint forms and letters for filing a complaint with your state attorney general. In some cases your complaint may be referred to another consumer complaint agency or site where you will be able to file a complaint on-line. The attorney general consumer complaint form can be filed over the internet, faxed or mailed.

List of State Attorney General Web Sites
http://www.fair-debt-collection.com/attorney-general.html

Alabama	Illinois	Montana	Rhode Island
Alaska	Indiana	Nebraska	South Carolina
Arizona	Iowa	Nevada	South Dakota
Arkansas	Kansas	New Hampshire	Tennessee
California	Kentucky	New Jersey	Texas
Colorado	Louisiana	New Mexico	Utah
Connecticut	Maine	New York	Vermont
Delaware	Maryland	North Carolina	Virginia
Florida	Massachusetts	North Dakota	Washington
DC (No website)	Michigan	Ohio	West Virginia
Georgia (No site)	Minnesota	Oklahoma	Wisconsin
Hawaii	Mississippi	Oregon	Wyoming
Idaho	Missouri	Pennsylvania	

How to Fight, Delay or Stop Foreclosures

Much of the information gathered in this section of was gleaned from reliable and useful resources, the most noteworthy of which was from the Consumer Warning Network. They can be found on the internet at ConsumerWarningNetwork.com. If you should be facing foreclosure, their content should be very well worth your time.

You should find that you will be able to find all the manuals, handbooks and legal forms on the Consumer Warning Network website in a matter of a few minutes. Most states are behind consumers who face foreclosure and a quick search on the internet will reveal this to be true. Be sure to check the resources available in your home state as a number of states also have free legal assistance for consumers facing foreclosure.

In short, you are not alone in your fight! If your state doesn't provide free legal assistance, the Consumer Warning Network manuals and handbooks provide fill-in-the-blank legal pleadings (forms) and instructions on exactly how to proceed on your own in and out of court. Thanks to Consumer Warning Network and other contributing organizations we can provide very useful overviews for fighting, delaying and, in some cases, completely stopping foreclosures.

Who Owns the Note?

The backbone of your strategy centers on a simple yet very powerful question. *"Who owns the promissory note you originally signed when you purchased your home?"* Your goal is to make certain the institution suing you is, in fact, the owner of the promissory note that **you** signed. There is only one original note for your mortgage which has your signature on it. This is the **only** document that can prove you owe the debt and the institution foreclosing on your home **must prove** that the debt you owe is now owed to them. Without the "original signed promissory note", the foreclosing institution does not have the standing (legal right) to foreclose on your loan; period.

During the lending boom, most mortgages were flipped and sold to another lender or sliced-up and sold to investors as securitized packages on Wall Street. In the rush to turn these over as fast as possible to make the most amount of money possible, many of the new lenders did not get the proper paperwork to show they own the note and mortgage. This is the key to your strategy. Now, many lenders are moving to foreclose on homeowners but don't have the proper paperwork to prove they have a right to foreclose on the note at all.

You Need to Challenge the Foreclosure If you don't challenge your lender, the court will simply allow the foreclosure to proceed. When you get a copy of the foreclosure suit many lenders automatically include a motion that the court re-establish the note (in their favor naturally). The motion often reads like this, *"...the Mortgage note has either been lost or destroyed and the Plaintiff is unable to state the manner in which this occurred."* In other words, they are admitting they don't have the note that proves they have a right to foreclose.

If the lender is allowed to proceed without that proof there is a possibility that other institutions which may have bought your note along the way, will also try to collect on the same debt from you again. Shocking as this may appear it has happened and you could face multiple foreclosures on the same promissory note! A Tennessee borrower recently had her lender, Ameriquest, foreclose on her in July and, about three months later, another bank sent her a default notice for the mortgage on the house she already lost in the previous foreclosure.

You Must Fight for Fairness This process is not intended to help you get your house for free. The primary goal is to delay the foreclosure and put pressure on the lender to negotiate. Despite all the hype about lenders wanting to help homeowners avoid foreclosure, most borrowers know that's not reality.

Steps to Undertake

What to Do if Your Lender has Already Filed Suit to Foreclose on Your Home?
First, use our foreclosure forms. It's a fill-in-the-blank legal request to your lender asking that the original note be produced before it can proceed with the foreclosure. In some states the courts require the original request to be filed with the clerk of court and a copy of the request to be sent to the attorney representing the lender. To find out the rules where you live, call the clerk of the court in the jurisdiction where you property is located.

If the lender's attorney does not respond within 30 days, file a motion to compel with the court and request that the court set a hearing on your motion. That, in effect, asks the judge to order the lender to produce the original documents.

The judge will issue a ruling at your hearing. Many judges around the country are becoming more sympathetic to homeowners because of the prevalence of predatory lending and servicing. In the past, many lenders have relied upon using lost note affidavits, but in many cases that's no longer enough to satisfy the judge. They are holding the lender to the letter of the law requiring them to produce evidence that they are the true owners of the note.

For example, as reported in the New York Times on the 15th of November 2007, Ohio Federal Court Judge Christopher Boyko dismissed 14 foreclosure cases in his ruling that the lenders failed to prove they owned the properties they were trying to seize.

"A federal district court in Ohio dismissed 14 foreclosure cases brought by Deutsche Bank (NYSE: DB) on behalf of mortgage investors because they couldn't produce proof that they owned the properties they were trying to seize, the New York Times reports today. These complicated mortgage securities, totaling $6.5 trillion of securitized mortgage debt as of the end of 2006, make it easy for investors to trade the securities, but harder for them to prove actual ownership in the courts.

Until this ruling, the courts have been letting them get away with it. They've also gotten away with the lax legal standards of proof because most people facing foreclosure don't have the money to fight lenders in court. Judge Boyko asked Deutsche Bank on October 10th to file copies of loan assignments showing that the lender was indeed the owner of the note and mortgage on each property when the foreclosure was filed. But the bank couldn't do that. It could only show that there was "intent" to convey the rights in the mortgages rather than proof of ownership. That's because to make things easier for the banks to buy and sell these securities the actual mortgage notes are not shipped around the world.

In fact sometimes an underlying mortgage can be put into more than one securitized debt package. Josh Rosner, a specialist in mortgage securities, told the Times, "I have heard instances where the same loan is in two or three pools." Katherine Porter, whose mortgage study was released last week, found that 40% of creditors foreclosing on borrowers did not show proof of ownership.

Judge Boyko decided to put an end to these lax legal practices and said in his ruling, "The institutions seem to adopt the attitude that since they have been doing this for so long, unchallenged, this practice equates with legal compliance. Finally put to the test, their weak legal arguments compel this court to stop them at the gate," according to the Times story."

New York Times
www.nytimes.com/2007/11/15/business/15lend.html?_r=0

United States vs. Northern District of Ohio
www.consumerwarningnetwork.com/wp-content/uploads/2008/06/judge-boyko-ruling1.pdf

What to Do if You are in Default but Your Lender has Not Yet Filed Suit Against You?
Use our foreclosure form requesting a copy of the promissory note, which is a fill-in-the-blank letter to your lender. This document requests the lender produce the original note before taking any foreclosure action against you. If the lender does not respond and files suit against you to foreclose, follow the steps previously described above requesting the lender 'produce the note' and then file a motion to compel, if necessary.

Mortgage Electronic Registration Systems (MERS)

MERS, which is an acronym for Mortgage Electronic Registration Systems, was created over a decade ago by several of the largest mortgage companies in America, including Fannie Mae, Freddie Mac, Wells Fargo, Citimortgage, Chase, HSBC and Countrywide (now owned by Bank of America).

During the peak of mortgage securitizations, when individual mortgages were repeatedly "sliced and diced" and sold as securities, the mortgage industry created MERS *"to streamline the mortgage process by acting as the mortgagee of record for the holders and servicers of mortgages"*.

In other words, MERS made it cheaper and faster for these mortgage companies to buy and sell loans without all the extra paperwork and fees they would have incurred had they done it the old fashioned way. The idea was that while your mortgage was being chopped up, sold and resold, the ownership interests would supposedly be electronically tracked by MERS, hopefully avoiding those pesky recording fees at the county records office.

But, for far too many people, MERS is a mystery company that forecloses on homes. Say a homeowner takes out a mortgage with Wells Fargo then, two years later, the homeowner gets behind in payments. That's when a foreclosure suit lands on the homeowners doorstep, but instead of Wells Fargo foreclosing someone named "MERS" is trying to take the home. If something like that has happened to you, at least now you will know who (or what) MERS "is".

Creating a Mortgage Monster By 2007, more than 50 million mortgages were registered with MERS. Since at least 2003 every HUD, Fannie Mae and Freddie Mac-backed mortgage has language nominating MERS as the mortgagee of record. With record numbers of mortgages going into foreclosure today, business for MERS is good. No matter how many times your mortgage might have been traded, MERS simplifies things for the mortgage industry by suing in the MERS name as a "nominee" of the actual mortgage company, whoever that may be. But here's the good news, MERS still has to prove it actually owns your loan!

Who Owns My Debt? The ability of MERS to foreclose in the name of the actual mortgage lender has been challenged in courts throughout the nation. Oftentimes, sloppy work by its attorneys causes MERS to get kicked out of court. In *California a court recently threw out foreclosure suits brought by MERS for failure to follow the rules as did a court in Nevada. **Rhode Island Attorney George Babcock has been very successful challenging the chain of title created by MERS. With all this 'precedence', maybe you can do the same!

*California
http://msnbcmedia.msn.com/i/msnbc/sections/news/JudgeBuffordsRuling.pdf

**Rhode Island Attorney George Babcock
http://www.consumerwarningnetwork.com/?s=george+babcock

Since MERS is merely an electronic database, it often has trouble proving it is the holder of the original promissory note. Just because MERS is suing you as the "nominee" for the lender doesn't excuse it from having to "produce the note" when demanded by the party being foreclosed on. If the original promissory note was not endorsed to MERS, MERS cannot foreclose. Some suits have failed because "lost note" affidavits (i.e., "we can't seem to find the actual signed note") have been rejected as insufficient.

Challenging a MERS Foreclosure

If your home is being foreclosed, and MERS appears as one of the parties involved in the lawsuit, you or your attorney should ask one or more of the following questions:

1. Does MERS have the original mortgage note in its possession?

2. Is MERS entitled to enforce the note as "nominee" of the actual mortgage company?

A "no" answer to either of these questions might mean that someone is improperly trying to take your property.

Interestingly, in Florida, MERS has already stopped the practice of trying to foreclose on homeowners in its own name. Why? Seems there's far too much opposition to MERS in Florida and it doesn't like the legal climate there.

When Your Lender Cannot Produce the Original Promissory Note

So, what happens when the lender tells the Court it can't produce the original note because it is lost? Let's start with the basics. If a lender wants to foreclose on a property, it has to be able to show that it is, in fact, the appropriate person or institution to whom the money is owed. The right to foreclose belongs **ONLY** to the person or institution who has the legitimate possession of the original promissory note; not a copy; not an electronic entry; but the original note itself showing the actual signatures of the person or persons who allegedly owes the money.

What Must the Lender Do?

Often what happens is that the lender claims it doesn't have the original note because that note has been lost or destroyed. The "Uniform Commercial Code" is a set of laws governing commercial transactions that many states, such as Florida, have adopted. It contains a specific provision on this subject (Section 3-309) which states that a person can enforce a promissory note without having the original, but only under certain limited circumstances.

Uniform Commercial Code Section 3-309
https://www.law.cornell.edu/ucc/3/article3

To be enforceable, **ALL** of the following must be proven by the lender:

1. The person has to claim that it no longer has the original note;

2. The person has to prove that it was properly in possession of the note and entitled to enforce it when it lost possession of the note;

3. The person has to prove it didn't "lose" possession simply because it transferred the note to someone else (i.e., it's not really lost); and

4. The person has to prove that it cannot produce the original note because the instrument was destroyed, or its whereabouts cannot be determined, or it was stolen by someone who had no right to it.

All of these matters have to be proven by the person trying to foreclose on the property. It is not the obligation of the borrower to prove or disprove any of this. The borrower can challenge the right of the person trying to foreclose and demand proof.

The Court's Important Role

It's up to the Court to determine whether the lender has satisfactorily explained why it can no longer produce the original note. The Court also has to be satisfied that when the original note was lost, the person trying to foreclose on the property had possession of the note at the time it was lost. Until the Court receives satisfactory answers the foreclosure cannot proceed.

It is also important for the Court to understand that this is not merely a "technicality" and the judge should not be satisfied with anything less than full proof of this issue. Why? Because the Court itself needs to appreciate the fact that if it agrees that the original note has been legitimately lost and it allows the foreclosure to proceed without the original note, it is the borrower who is still at risk from foreclosure proceedings from other so called "note holders".

How to use "Produce the Note" in Non-Judicial Foreclosure States

In some states, a lender can foreclose on your home without going to court. These are called non-judicial foreclosure states. You can still use the same strategy in these states, but it takes a few more steps on your part.

First, the concept behind "Produce the Note" is that when a homeowner is faced with a foreclosure suit, "Produce the Note" requires the lender to prove it has the authority to foreclose by requiring it to officially produce the original promissory note in the lawsuit. But if there is no foreclosure lawsuit, what can homeowners do? In these non-judicial foreclosure states such as California, Texas, and 30 or more other states with similar procedures, the homeowner has to file a lawsuit against the party trying to foreclose.

List of Non-Judicial Foresclosure States
http://www.all-foreclosure.com/help/procedures.htm

In a state with non-judicial foreclosure procedures, a foreclosure sale can be initiated by the lender without using court proceedings.

1. Homeowners receive a "Notice of Intent" letter informing them that a foreclosure sale will be scheduled unless the overdue debt is paid within a certain amount of time.

2. If the debt is not paid accordingly, a "Notice of Sale" is then sent informing the homeowner that a foreclosure sale will take place at a particular time and place.

3. No lawsuit is ever initiated by the lender and the courts are not involved.

4. Without a lawsuit, you cannot use judicial procedures to require the lender to "produce the note."

NOTE Merely sending a private letter to the lender "demanding" that it produce the original note to the borrower may be met with utter disregard or outright refusal by the lender.

Produce the Note

In a non-judicial foreclosure state, in order to protect yourself, by demanding that the lender "produce the note," it will be necessary for you to first file your own lawsuit. Even in such non-judicial foreclosure states, no law prohibits you from instituting your own lawsuit challenging the right of a lender to foreclose on your property. The lawsuit would allege that:

1. The lender has sent a Notice of Intent to Foreclose;

2. The homeowner is unsure as to whether the lender still possesses the original debt instrument upon which the lender claims the right to foreclose;

3. The homeowner wants proof of such authority and requests the court intervene and prevent the foreclosure from taking place unless and until such proof is presented.

Initiating litigation to protect your rights is never a simple process. Requirements as to what must be contained in a pleading, how the facts must be plead, who should be named in the pleading, and how the pleading should be officially "served" on the lender all differ from state to state.

Remember, most states 'go to bat' for consumers who face foreclosure. Your state more than likely offers references to free legal help and manuals or handbooks, some even provide "fill-in-the-blanks" legal pleadings (forms) on how to proceed on your own in and out of court. Use these free references as they are often extremely helpful.

Once a lawsuit is initiated, however, all states have judicial procedures that allow a party to require the other side to produce relevant documents and the "produce the note" strategy can be used.

How to Produce the Note

http://www.consumerwarningnetwork.com/2008/06/19/produce-the-note-how-to

Additionally, go online and research the key phrase "Request for Production of Documents" and you should find many sample court pleading formats available from multiple states. it's very easy to copy, paste and prepare those documents if you have no attorney assisting you.

Finally, there are usually "legal aid" organizations around set up to assist individuals who may have difficulty paying for the services of an attorney. Good luck and excercise your rights!

Agreements, Forms and Letters

AssetProtectionServices.com

Request for Temporary Payment Plan
(Creditor)

Date
Your Name, Address and Telephone Number
Your Social Security Number

Re: Account Number

Creditor's Name
Department
Creditor's Address

Dear Sir or Madam,

This letter is a written request for a temporary change in the repayment terms of my debt account. I am currently going through financial crisis and may not be able to follow the current payment plan. Neither do I plan to file a bankruptcy nor do I intend to default on this debt.

I do have some income from *<mention income sources>*. However, when I examined my financial situation and planned a budget, it became necessary for me to request each of my creditors to accept a reduced/alternative payment plan for a number of months (*specify the number, if possible*).

I would appreciate your co-operation in making this payment plan effective shortly. I request you to accept a monthly payment of $_____ instead of the regular payments of $_____ made on the *<date>* of each month. I hereby assure you that I shall not add to my debt till my financial situation improves.

I shall begin making regular monthly payments as soon as I recover from this financial crisis. I hope you will understand my situation and co-operate with me. I shall surely notify you of any change in my financial situation.

Your co-operation during this difficult time is highly appreciated.

Respectfully,

<Your Signature>
<Your Printed Name>

Request for Reduced Payment Plan
(Creditor)

Date
Your Name, Address and Telephone Number
Your Social Security Number

Re: Account Number

Creditor's Name
Department
Creditor's Address

Dear Sir or Madam,

I am presently going through some financial difficulties and fear that I will not be able to meet my monthly payments to you. I do not want to declare bankruptcy and want to try and work out a payment plan so that I don't have to default on this debt.

(*Relate your financial trouble, only as much is required for official purposes*)

I would like to suggest a strategy which may be acceptable. If you would, close my account, waive the interest payments and accept a new balance of $_____$, instead of what I currently owe, then I can afford to make a monthly payment in the amount of $_____$.

I am sure you will agree to the situation which has caused this fallout. Please feel free to have one of your representatives call me and work out the final strategy.

If you feel you can't adjust the payment plan, I would be forced to default on this account. I intend only to pay creditors who can work with me. Thanks for your kind consideration.

Respectfully,

<Your Signature>
<Your Printed Name>

Proposal for Reduced Debt Settlement In-Full
(Creditor)

Date
Your Name, Address and Telephone Number
Your Social Security Number

Re: Account Number

Creditor's Name
Department
Creditor's Address

Dear Sir or Madam,

I am presently going through financial difficulties and will not be able to meet my monthly obligation to you as well as my other creditors. I do not want to declare bankruptcy but instead would propose a settlement of my debt with you.

The amount that I propose to pay in order to settle the debt with you *in full* is $_____.
As part of this settlement, I request that you remove any negative entries (late payments, charge offs, etc) relating to this account which you may have placed on my credit report.

Please note that currently I am negotiating with other creditors as well. Unfortunately, I do not have enough funds to pay all of my creditors so time is of the essence here.

Please note that initially I will only be able to pay those creditors who are willing to work with me. In addition, at this point I am not sure how long I will have funds available in order to satisfy my creditors; therefore please respond to my proposal as soon as you can.

If you find my settlement offer acceptable, please forward me a letter (on your company letterhead) confirming that your company is agreeable to my requests as outlined above. Once I receive a signed and acknowledged letter from a person authorized to accept my settlement offer from your company, I shall forward you certified funds in the amount stated above.

Your co-operation during this difficult time is highly appreciated.

Respectfully,

<Your Signature>
<Your Printed Name>

Counter-Offer Settlement
(Creditor)

Date
Your Name, Address and Telephone Number
Your Social Security Number

Re: Account Number

Creditor's Name
Department
Creditor's Address

Dear Sir or Madam,

I appreciate that your company is willing to work with me in settling my debt and paying it off.

This letter is to make a counter offer in response to the settlement offer made by your customer service representative (*put in person's name*) on (*date*).

The amount that I would propose to settle the debt in full is $_____. However, as part of this offer, I would request that you to remove any late payment entry or charge-offs on this account from my credit report.

I would also like to inform you that I have other outstanding debts with other creditors and unfortunately, only very limited funds available to pay the creditors. Therefore, I can pay only those creditors who are willing to meet my terms. I have already reached agreeable settlements with some of these creditors and I doubt whether I'll have enough funds to pay everyone.

If your company is willing to accept my proposal, please sign the attached letter of agreement and return a copy of the same to me. As soon as I receive this signed acknowledged agreement, I shall send you the money order in the amount I've proposed.

Respectfully,

<Your Signature>
<Your Printed Name>

Debt Settlement Agreement
(Creditor)

Date
Your Name, Address and Telephone Number
Your Social Security Number

Re: Account Number

Creditor's Name
Department
Creditor's Address

Dear Sir or Madam,

<Creditor's Name>, the Creditor's Representative and *<Your Name>*, the Debtor agree to settle the debt in the amount of $_____ under the following terms and conditions:

The Creditor and Debtor agree that the current outstanding debt is $_____. Both parties agree that the Creditor will accept a cash payment of $_____ in full settlement of the debt.

The Creditor agrees to compromise the debt under the condition that he'll receive the said payment by certified funds within 20 days from the date of this acceptance.

The parties hereto agree that should Debtor fail to provide the amount stated herein by certified funds within 20 days from the date of this acceptance, the Creditor shall immediately demand the payment of the original amount owed by the Debtor.

The undersigned also declares that he/she is authorized to act as an agent of the Creditor's company and that this agreement for debt settlement shall be binding upon the Creditor, Debtor and their individual successors and assignees.

Signature: _____ Date: _____

Debtor's name: _____

Signature: _____ Date: _____

Creditor's name: _____

Release and Settlement Agreement
(Creditor)

RELEASE AND SETTLEMENT AGREEMENT

This **RELEASE AND SETTLEMENT AGREEMENT** (*hereinafter "Agreement"*) is entered into this the _____ day of _____, 20___ by and between:

Name: _____

Mailing Address: _____

_____

(hereinafter referred to as "**Debtor**")

Name: _____

Mailing Address: _____

_____

(hereinafter referred to as the "**Creditor**"), collectively hereinafter referred to as the "**Parties**".

1. **DISPUTE** A dispute has arisen over the payment of purchases, invoices for goods and/or services and/or other debt obligations between the Parties.

2. **DESIRE TO SETTLE** The Parties desire to settle this dispute and to settle their differences as to their rights, duties and obligations, each arising from the subject matter of this Agreement.

3. **AGREEMENT TO PAY** Debtor hereby agrees to pay to Creditor concurrent with or after his/her/their execution of this Agreement, the sum of _____ ($_____) dollars, in the form of a cashier's check or other certified funds.

4. **LEGAL PROCEEDING OR LIEN** In the event that Creditor has filed, or had filed, any form of legal proceedings and/or liens of any kind against Debtor, the Creditor, in consideration of the payment articulated in Paragraph 3 above, hereby agrees to fully discharge such lien and/or withdraw any and all legal proceedingss pertaining thereto.

5. **FULL AND FINAL RELEASE** Creditor, on behalf of it's agents, heirs, executors, administrators, successors and assigns, hereby fully releases and discharges Debtor and his/her/their heirs, successors, executors, administrators, its agents, servants, shareholders, employees, representatives and assigns from any and all claims, debts, liabilities, demands, obligations, costs, expenses, damages, actions and causes of action, of whatever kind or

nature, whether known or unknown, based on, rising out of, or in connection with anything whatsoever done, omitted or suffered to be done, at any time prior to the date of this Agreement.

6. **REPRESENTATIVES AND WARRANTIES** Creditor hereby represents, warrants, and guarantees that he/she/it is the true and lawful creditor of Debtor and that to their knowledge, no other person or entity has any right title or interest whatsoever in the above referenced debt. In addition, Creditor represents, warrants, and guarantees that upon receipt of the payment herein referenced, Creditor agrees to consider the above referenced account to be settled in full and shall report the same to the proper credit-reporting agencies (*if applicable*), immediately upon the payment clearing their bank.

7. **LIABILITY** This settlement is the compromise of a disputed claim as set forth in this Agreement and shall never be treated as an admission of liability by either party for any reason or purpose whatsoever.

8. **INDEMNIFICATION** Once Creditor has accepted the payment from Debtor, Creditor hereby agrees to indemnify, hold harmless and pay any legal defense costs of Debtor from any loss, claim, lien, expense, demand or cause of action of any kind, asserted by any third-party to a claim connected with the subject matter of this Agreement.

CREDITOR'S ACCEPTANCE & RELEASE:

Signed: _____   Title: _____

Printed Name: _____   Date Signed: ____/_____/20___

DEBTOR'S ACCEPTANCE & RELEASE:

Signed: _____

Printed Name: _____   Date Signed: ____/_____/20___

Signed: _____

Printed Name: _____   Date Signed: ____/_____/20___

Expired Statute of Limitations Notification
(Creditor)

Date
Your Name, Address and Telephone Number
Your Social Security Number

Re: Account Number

Creditor's Name
Department
Creditor's Address

Dear Sir or Madam,

This letter is in response to your letter dated <Date> (copy attached) or phone call dated <Date> regarding the collection you are attempting on the account number stated above.

I do not believe that I owe this debt and therefore I dispute that this is a valid account. I am aware of my rights under the Fair Debt Collection Practices Act (FDCPA) and my state laws.

Therefore, I would like to inform you that I have checked with my State Attorney General and verified that the Statute of Limitations for this type of debt through the courts in <State in which contract was signed> has expired. If you intend to attempt to take this issue to court, be advised that I shall inform the court that I have disputed this debt and that the Statute of Limitations has expired.

Therefore, this letter is to demand that neither you nor anyone affiliated with your company contact me except to inform that all collection efforts are terminated or that you or the creditor you claim to represent are taking actions allowed by the FDCPA and/or my state laws.

Henceforth, I shall consider any contact from anyone connected with your company to be in violation of The Fair Debt Collection Practices Act (FDCPA) and I will immediately report it to the State Attorney General and/or Federal Trade Commission.

Be further advised that I tape record all phone calls and violations of the FDCPA can result in you or the company being fined up to $1,000 per incident.

Respectfully,

<Your Signature>
<Your Printed Name>

Request to Stop Contact
(Collection Agency)

Date
Your Name and Address
Your Social Security Number

Re: Company Name
     Account Number

Collection Agency's Name
Collection Agency's Address

Dear Collection Manager,

This letter is my demand that you stop contacting me in order to collect payments on the account stated above. I am **ONLY** interested in working out a settlement plan with the original creditor.

Therefore, I hereby instruct you to stop **ALL** collection efforts immediately or face possible legal action under state and federal laws.

Respectfully,

<Your Signature>
<Your Printed Name>

Notice to Cease and Desist
(Collection Agency)

Date
Your Name and Address
Your Social Security Number

Re: Company Name
        Account Number

Collection Agency's Name
Collection Agency's Address

Dear Collection Manager,

This letter is a written notice to cease and desist in your efforts to collect on the debt account as stated above. It is my personal choice to deal directly with the original creditor and not any collection agencies.

Thus, I request you cease and desist collection efforts immediately or face legal actions under state and federal laws. I entrust you will give careful consideration to this letter and heed my warning.

Respectfully,

<Your Signature>
<Your Printed Name>

Notice and Demand to Immediately Cease and Decist
(Collection Agency)

Date
Your Name and Address
Your Social Security Number

Re: Company Name
      Account Number

Collection Agency's Name
Collection Agency's Address

Dear Collection Manager,

I, the above named person, am formally notifying your company that I deny ever having a debt with the company you claim I owe and am therefore demanding you immediately Cease and Desist any and all collection actions against me unless, within the next thirty (30) days, your company provides me with a copy of a **CONTRACT SIGNED BY ME** obligating me to pay money on the account with the company to whom you claim I am indebted.

Further, you are hereby notified under the provisions of Public Law 95-109, Section 805-C of the Fair Debt Collection Practices Act, to **CEASE AND DESIST** in any and all attempts to collect any so called debts from me based on the account and/or on behalf of the creditor named herein unless and until you formally "validate" (not verify) the said debt.

In addition, you are advised that NO derogatory (*dictionary definition is to be used to determine the scope of this word*) information is to be placed on any credit reports or with any credit-reporting agencies after your receipt of this **Notice and Demand to Immediately Cease and Desist**. In addition, absent the contract referenced above, I hereby demand that you formally rescind any derogatory information you have previously been a party to placing on my credit reports relating to the above referenced account (if any).

YOUR FAILURE TO CEASE AND DESIST AS DIRECTED HEREIN SHALL RESULT IN CHARGES BEING FILED AGAINST YOUR COMPANY WITH STATE AND FEDERAL REGULATORY AGENCIES EMPOWERED TO REGULATE YOUR INDUSTRY.

Be Warned, Your Future Actions Will Determine my Response!

Respectfully,
<Your Signature>
<Your Printed Name>

Debt Validation
(Collection Agency)

YOUR LETTERHEAD

Date
Your Name and Address
Your Social Security Number

Re: Alleged Creditor's Name
     Alleged Creditor's Address
     Alleged Account Number

Collection Agency's Name
Collection Agency's Address

Dear Collection Manager,

This letter is being sent to you in response to a letter I received from you dated _____, which was received at my mailing address on _____.

Your letter is unsatisfactory as proof that I owe the alleged debt (see Fields v. Wilber Law Firm, Donald L. Wilber and Kenneth Wilber, USCA-02-C-0072, 7th Circuit Court, Sept 2004.).

You are hereby put on notice that should you continue to contact me or move forward in **any way** without first properly **validating** the alleged debt pursuant to the requirements stated in this letter, I shall consider it harassment and shall file complaints with the appropriate regulatory agencies and file a small claims action against you personally and your company.

This is NOT a request for "verification" or proof of my mailing address, but is a DEMAND for VALIDATION. I am requiring that you validate this debt according to the Fair Debt Collections Practices Act.

In order for you to have the opportunity to properly **validate** this alleged debt, I am allowing you an additional 30 days from the date of this letter to **provide me ALL of the following**:

1. Explain and show me how you calculated what you say I owe.

2. **Provide complete copies of any and all documents and/or other papers that bears my orignal signature and shows I have formally agreed to pay what you say I owe (i.e "Show Me the Original Contract").**

3. Provide a verified copy of any judgment, if applicable.

4. Identify the original creditor.

5. **Provide proof that you are licensed to collect a debt in my state.**

6. **Provide me with your license numbers and registered agent in my state**.

Also, during this period, if any action is taken which could be considered detrimental to me on any of my credit reports, I will consult with my legal counsel for suit as well as filing formal complaints with the attorney General of my state, your state, all major credit-reporting agencies and the Federal Trade Commission (FTC). Your actions include any information you may have sent to a credit-reporting repository that is disputed, could be inaccurate, invalidated, or where you verified an account as accurate *when in fact there is no valid proof provided by you that this alleged debt is actually owed by me*.

Unless you **provide a copy of the alleged contract with my signature on it and the information required above within the time I have allocated to you, you MUST immediately cease and desist** all future actions regarding this matter and remove any and all collection listings from my credit report(s) that you may have filed.

Should you fail to do so, you will be subject to a lawsuit for violation of FDCPA § 809(b) and should your offices attempt any further communication with me or any third-parties concerning me it will be considered harassment and I will have no choice but to file a complaint with the attorney General of my state, your state, all major credit-reporting agencies and the Federal Trade Commission (FTC).

I strongly advise you to be very sure that your records are in order and that you properly **VALIDATE** *(not just attempt to Verify)* the alleged debt before you proceed further or I will be forced to take legal action against you.

Your future actions will determine the future course I will undertake. Choose wisely.

Respectfully,

<Your Signature>
<Your Printed Name>

Debt Validation - No Reply
(Collection Agency)

Date
Your Name and Address
Your Social Security Number

Re: Company Name
     Account Number

Collection Agency's Name
Collection Agency's Address

Dear Collection Manager,

I have sent your company a written request for validation of the debt you allege that I owe having the account number referenced above on *<Date>*. According to the Fair Debt Collection Practices Act (FDCPA) I have the right to require the **validation** of this debt and, once validation is requested, you are obliged to provide relevant documentation before you may carry on any collection activities regarding this debt. Unfortunately, I have **not** received a reply from you except the confirmation (by mail) that you did receive my request for validation of debt on *<Date>*.

As per an opinion letter published by the FTC reporting this collection to a credit-reporting agency is considered a collection activity. Therefore, I hereby notify you that you are now in violation of the FDCPA and subject to a fine of $1,000 which I can collect from you by simply filing a claim in my local small claims court against your company. Further, be advised that I intend to follow through with the claim if I don't receive proper validation of this alleged debt as per my previous written request for validation from you within the next 15 calendar days.

This letter is intended to remind you that reporting such invalidated information to any credit-reporting agency can result in defamation of my character, as any negative listing on my credit report would adversely affect my credit. I further recommend that you immediately consult with your legal counsel concerning your non-compliance as this request could lead your company into serious legal problems with litigation (in small claims court), the FTC and other state and federal agencies.

BE WARNED, YOUR FUTURE ACTIONS WILL DETERMINE MY FUTURE RESPONSE!

Respectfully,
<Your Signature>
<Your Printed Name>

Debt Validation - Response
(Collection Agency)

NOTICE OF INSUFFICIENT VALIDATION

Date
Your Name and Address
Your Social Security Number

Re: Company Name
     Account Number

Collection Agency's Name
Collection Agency's Address

Dear Collection Manager,

This letter is being sent to you in response to a letter I received from you dated _____, which was received on _____, to inform you that you have *not* in any way validated the debt that you allege I owe according to 15 USC §1692g.

Your response letter is totally unsatisfactory as proof that I owe the alleged debt (see Fields v. Wilber Law Firm, Donald L. Wilber and Kenneth Wilber, USCA-02-C-0072, 7th Circuit Court, Sept 2004.). Additionally, in no way have you complied with my right to have the debt validated according to the standards of the FDCPA, and *your response is hereby rejected.*

You are hereby put on notice that should you continue to contact me or move forward in *any way* without first properly *validating* the alleged debt pursuant to the requirements stated in this letter and my previous letter dated _____, I shall consider it as harassment and shall immediately file complaints with the appropriate regulatory agencies and file a small claims action against your company.

*This is NOT a request for "verification" or proof of my mailing address,
but is a __DEMAND__ for __VALIDATION__. I am requiring that you validate
this debt according to the Fair Debt Collections Practices Act.*

In order for you to have the opportunity to properly *validate* this alleged debt, I am allowing you an additional 10 days from the date of this letter to *provide me ALL of the following*:

1. Explain and show me how you calculated what you say I owe.

2. **Provide complete copies of any and all documents and/or other papers that bears my orignal signature and shows I have formally agreed to pay what you say I owe (i.e "Show Me the Original Contract").**

3.   Provide a verified copy of any judgment, if applicable.

4.   Identify the original creditor.

5.   **Provide proof that you are licensed to collect a debt in my state.**

6.   **Provide me with your license numbers and registered agent in my state**.

Also, during this period, if any action is taken which could be considered detrimental to me on any of my credit reports, I will consult with my legal counsel for suit as well as filing formal complaints with the attorney General of my state, your state, all major credit-reporting agencies and the Federal Trade Commission (FTC). Your actions include any information you may have sent to a credit-reporting repository that is disputed, could be inaccurate, invalidated, or where you verified an account as accurate *when in fact there is no valid proof provided by you that this alleged debt is actually owed by me*.

Unless you **provide a copy of the alleged contract with my signature on it and the information required above within the time I have allocated to you, you MUST immediately cease and desist** all future actions regarding this matter and remove any and all collection listings from my credit report(s) that you may have filed.

Should you fail to do so, you will be subject to a lawsuit for violation of FDCPA § 809(b) and should your offices attempt any further communication with me or any third-parties concerning me it will be considered harassment and I will have no choice but to file a complaint with the attorney General of my state, your state, all major credit-reporting agencies and the Federal Trade Commission (FTC).

I strongly advise you to be very sure that your records are in order and that you properly **VALIDATE** *(not just attempt to Verify)* the alleged debt before you proceed further or I will be forced to take legal action against you.

   Your future actions will determine the future course I will undertake. Choose wisely.

Respectfully,

<Your Signature>
<Your Printed Name>

Remove Inquiries
(Credit-Reporting Agency)

Date
Your Name and Address
Your Social Security Number

Re: Remove Inquiry

Credit-Reporting Agency's Name
Credit-Reporting Agency's Address

Dear Sir or Madam,

This letter is a formal complaint that you are reporting inaccurate or incomplete credit information.

I am distressed that you have included the below information in my credit profile and have failed to maintain reasonable procedures in your operations to assure maximum possible accuracy in the credit reports you publish.

Credit-Reporting laws ensure that bureaus report only 100% accurate credit information. Every step must be taken to assure the information reported is completely accuratet.

The following information therefore needs to be reinvestigated. I respectfully request to be provided proof that these inquiries were in fact authorized with an instrument bearing my signature and for legitimate business purposes. Failing that, the unauthorized inquiry must be deleted from the report as soon as possible:

Re: Company Name:
       Account Number:

The listed inquiry was without authorization and, as near as I can see, for no reasonable business purposes. As such, it is a serious error in reporting. Please delete this misleading information and supply a corrected credit profile to me immediately. Under federal law you have 30 days to complete your reinvestigation and respond to my inquiry.

Thank you in advance for your cooperation in this matter.

Respectfully,
<Your Signature>
<Your Printed Name>

Dispute Accuracy of Account Information
(Credit-Reporting Agency)

Date
Your Name and Address
Your Social Security Number

Re: Company Name
       Account Number

Credit-Reporting Agency's Name
Credit-Reporting Agency's Address

Dear Sir or Madam,

I am writing to dispute the account referenced above. I have disputed this account information as inaccurate with you and you have responded stating that you were able to verify this debt. How is this possible? Under the laws of the FDCPA, I have contacted the collection agency named above myself and have been unable to get them to validate that this is indeed my debt.

I herewith enclose copies of my requests to the collection agency, asking them to validate my debts, and the receipts showing that I sent these letter certified signature requested. This debt is not mine and I was given no evidence of my obligation to pay this debt to this collection agency.

The FCRA requires you to verify the validity of the item within 30 days. If the validity can not be verified, you are obligated by law to remove the item from my credit report. There is a clear case of invalidated debt and I urge you to remove this item before I'm forced to take action against you with various state and federal agencies having oversight in your industry.

In the event that you cannot or will not properly validate the item pursuant to the FCRA, and you continue to list the disputed item on my credit report I will find it necessary to sue you for actual damages and declaratory relief under the FCRA. According to this regulation, I may sue you in any qualified state or federal court, including small claims court in my area.

I look forward to your resolution of this matter.

Respectfully,

<Your Signature>
<Your Printed Name>

Failure to Respond Timely
(Credit-Reporting Agency)

Date
Your Name and Address
Your Social Security Number

Credit-Reporting Agency's Name
Credit-Reporting Agency's Address

Dear Sir or Madam,

This letter is formal notice that you have failed to respond in a timely manner to my dispute letter of _____, deposited by registered mail with the Post Office on that date.

As you are well aware, federal law requires you to respond within 30 days, yet you have failed to respond. Failure to comply with these federal regulations by credit-reporting agencies are investigated by the Federal Trade Commission (*see 15 USC 41, et seq.*). I am maintaining a careful record of my communications with you on this matter for the purpose of filing a complaint with the FTC should you continue in your non-compliance.

For your benefit, and as a gesture of my goodwill, I will restate my dispute. The following information needs to be validated and deleted from the report as soon as possible:

Re: Company Name:
     Account Number:

The listed item is completely inaccurate and/or incomplete, and is a very serious error in reporting. Please delete this misleading information, and supply a corrected credit profile to me immediately.

Under federal law, you had 30 days to complete your reinvestigation, yet you have failed to respond. Do not delay further. Therefore, be aware that I am making a final goodwill attempt to have you clear up this matter. You have an additional 15 days from your receipt of this letter to cure this malady.

Respectfully,

<Your Signature>
<Your Printed Name>

Debt Verification vs. Debt Validation
(Credit-Reporting Agency)

Date
Your Name and Address
Your Social Security Number

Re: Company Name
     Account Number

Credit-Reporting Agency's Name
Credit-Reporting Agency's Address

Dear Sir or Madam,

This letter is to dispute the debt account referenced above. There is a serious mis-understanding with the collection agency claiming that this debt is owed by me. How were you able to "verify" this debt when the collection agency has not been able to "validate" that I owe this debt? I contend this debt is not mine and have demanded validation accordingly.

I am enclosing copies of the written requests that I have sent to the collection agency wherein I requested they validate this debt. I'm also attaching receipts showing they have received these letters.

As per the FCRA, you need to verify the validity of this item within 30 days. If you cannot verify the validity of this debt, you are obligated by the law to remove this item before I am forced to take legal action through my local small claims court and the state and federal agencies regulating your company for unlawful practices of this collection agency.

In case you cannot verify the item as required by the FCRA, and you continue to list the disputed item on my credit report, I may find it necessary to sue you for actual damages and declaratory relief under the FCRA. According to this regulation I may sue you in a qualified state or federal court including small claims court in my area.

While I would prefer to not litigate, I may use the courts as required to enforce my rights under the FCRA.

BE WARNED, YOUR FUTURE ACTIONS WILL DETERMINE MY FUTURE RESPONSE!

Respectfully,
<Your Signature>
<Your Printed Name>

Notice to Remove Inaccurate Information
(Credit-Reporting Agency)

Date
Your Name and Address
Your Social Security Number

Re: Company Name
       Account Number

Credit-Reporting Agency's Name
Credit-Reporting Agency's Address

Dear Sir or Madam,

I've just reviewed my credit report and have noticed there are the following inaccurate items on my credit report:

Name: _____   Acct: _____
This account is listed as being _____ days late, however, I have never been late on this account.

Name: _____   Acct: _____
This account is listed as a "charge off" however I have never had an account with this company.

In addition, there are other accounts which have been inactive for more than 7 years. As you know, the FCRA states that all credit older than 7 years should be removed from my credit report. The following accounts should therefore be removed:

Name: _____   Acct: _____
Name: _____   Acct: _____
Name: _____   Acct: _____

I have enclosed a copy of my driver's license as proof of identity.

Your co-operation with this matter is highly appreciated.

Respectfully,

<Your Signature>
<Your Printed Name>

Remove Inaccurate Information
(Credit-Reporting Agency)

Date
Your Name and Address
Your Social Security Number

Re: Company Name
        Account Number

Credit-Reporting Agency's Name
Credit-Reporting Agency's Address

Dear Sir or Madam,

In reviewing my credit bureau report from your agency, I have found an error regarding the following account, which has been inaccurately reported.

Company:
Account Number:

Under the provisions set forth in the Federal Fair Credit-Reporting Act, I hereby request that your agency prove the accuracy of the abovementioned account to me (in writing). Additionally, as I know you are aware, under the terms of the Act and succeeding court cases your agency has only thirty (30) days from your receipt of this letter to prove the accuracy of the above account or remove it entirely from my credit report.

Please note that this letter was sent via certified mail, and that I expect your written response within said thirty-(30) days. Should I not receive your response timely, I will immediately exercise all remedies available to me under the Act and/or other federal and state regulations relating to your failure to comply with the laws that regulate your industry.

Please feel free to contact me if you have any questions regarding this matter. I can be reached via e-mail at <your e-mail address here>. Your co-operation during this difficult time is highly appreciated.

Respectfully,

<Your Signature>
<Your printed name>

Demand to Remove Inaccurate Information on Credit Report
(Credit-Reporting Agency)

WRITTEN DEMAND TO REMOVE
INACCURATE INFORMATION ON CREDIT REPORT

Date
Your Name and Address
Your Social Security Number

Re: Company Name
     Account Number

Credit-Reporting Agency's Name
Credit-Reporting Agency's Address

Dear Sir or Madam,

As I have stated in my previous requests (sent by certified or registered mail), while reviewing my credit report from your agency I have found an error regarding the following alleged account, which I assert is being inaccurately reported.

Alleged Creditor Company:
Alleged Account Number:

Under the provisions set forth in the Federal Fair Credit-Reporting Act (hereinafter "Act"), I hereby **FORMALLY DEMAND** that your agency prove the accuracy of the abovementioned account to me in-writing or remove the entry from my credit report. I assert that I have not contracted with this self-proclaimed creditor for any reason and therefore couldn't owe them the money that they claim I owe them.

Further, absent proof that the debt is actually mine your agency **MUST** remove the entry from my credit report according to the Act.

Additionally, as I know you are aware, under the terms of the Act, and succeeding court cases, your agency has only thirty (30) days from your receipt of this letter to prove the accuracy of the above account or remove it entirely from my credit report. This self-proclaimed creditor simply stating that I owe them money, commonly referred to as "verification of debt", *is not valid proof*. A signed contract is the ***ONLY validating proof***. Absent that, then this entry **MUST** be removed by law.

Be advised that this letter represents my **LAST ATTEMPT** to request that your company abide by the Act and the laws governing your agency. If you do not properly "validate" or remove this inaccurate and/or incomplete information within the thirty (30) days allowed under the law, I shall file formal complaints with the FTC and all other regulatory agencies that have oversight over your industry.

Furthermore, I intend to seek redress in a small claims action for recovery of damages, costs, and attorney's fees should you continue in your deliberate obstruction of the law. For this purpose I am carefully documenting these events, including your lack of response as **REQUIRED** under law.

BE WARNED, YOU'RE FUTURE ACTIONS WILL DETERMINE MY FUTURE RESPONSE!

If needed, you may contact me if you have any questions regarding this matter. Additionally, I can be reached via e-mail at _____.

Respectfully,

<Your Signature>
<Your Printed Name>

Notice of Intent to File Complaint
(Credit-Reporting Agency)

NOTICE OF INTENT TO FILE COMPLAINT

Date
Your Name and Address
Your Social Security Number

Credit-Reporting Agency's Name
Credit-Reporting Agency's Address

Dear Sir or Madam,

This letter shall serve as formal Notice of Intent to file a Complaint with the FTC, due to your blatant disregard for the law.

As indicated by the attached copies of letters and mailing receipts delivered by registered mail both a dispute letter, dated _____, as well as a follow-up letter, dated _____. As of this moment, you have not done your duty mandated under the law. Your inaction in this matter is inexcusable and your disregard for the law is contemptible. Rest assured I will hold you to account.

For the record, the following information is being erroneously included on my credit report, as I have advised you on two separate occasions, more than _____ days ago and again _____ days ago:

Re: Company Name:
     Account Number:

If you do not immediately remove this inaccurate and incomplete information, I will file a formal complaint with the FTC. Furthermore, I intend to seek redress in a small claims action, for recovery of damages, costs and attorney's fees, should you continue in your deliberate obstruction of the law. For this purpose, I am carefully documenting these events, including your lack of response as REQUIRED under law.

Respectfully,

<Your Signature>
<Your Printed Name>

Request for Copy of Original Promissory Note
(Foreclosures)

Date
Your Name and Address
Your Social Security Number

Re: Request for Copy of Promissory Note

Creditor's Name
Creditor's Address

Property Address: [address of property subject to mortgage]
Loan Number: _____

Dear ,

I am the owner of certain real property located at <property address>, which is

security for a loan made by <company which issued loan> to me on <date on loan>.

Please produce for my inspection within ten (1) days the Original Promissory Note

which I signed on <date note was signed>.

If you have any questions regarding my request, please call me at <your phone
number>.

Respectfully,

<Your Signature>
<Your Printed Name>

Defendant's Motion to Compel
(Foreclosures)

IN THE COURT OF _____ IN AND FOR

_____ COUNTY, STATE OF _____

CIVIL DIVISION

_____,   CASE NO.: _____

<Name of Lender>

        Plaintiff

vs.

_____,

<Your Name>

        Defendant

DEFENDANT'S MOTION TO COMPEL

Defendant <your name>, moves the court for the entry of an Order directing Plaintiff to produce to Defendant the document described in the REQUEST FOR PRODUCTION OF DOCUMENT which is attached as an exhibit to this action. The basis for the relief requested is set forth below.

On <date of request to produce to Plaintiff's lawyer>, Defendant sent to Plaintiff's Counsel by U.S. Mail the request to produce, a copy of which is attached as an exhibit.

Despite the passage of 30 days (in addition to 5 days, as this request was sent by U.S. Mail for the services of Plaintiff's counsel*) of this request on Plaintiff's counsel, Plaintiff has not produced the requested document to Defendant or contacted Defendant to state that the document is available for inspection and copying.

*Note Delete the following passage before filing:

"You should check the Rules of Procedure in your jurisdiction or call the Clerk of Court to confirm how much time a litigant has to respond to Discovery before you can Move to Compel the production of this document. Thirty (30) days has been inserted in the Motion as this is the amount of time most states give a litigant to respond. Your state's rules may be different, and you need to state in the Motion the number of days which your state provides."

Defendant hereby requests that this court enter an Order directing Plaintiff to produce the

document requested by Defendant in the REQUEST FOR PRODUCTION OF DOCUMENT,

and provide to Defendant such other and further relief to which Defendant may be justly

entitled to under the circumstances.

<Sign Your Name>
<Print Your Name>
<Print Your Address>

CERTIFICATE OF SERVICE

I HEREBY CERTIFY that a true and correct copy of the above and foregoing has been

furnished by U.S. Mail to [name and address of Plaintiff / Bank or Mortgage Company], this

_____ day of _____, 20___.

<Sign Your Name>
<Print Your Name>

Request for Production of Document
(Foreclosures)

IN THE CIRCUIT COURT OF _____ JUDICIAL CIRCUIT

IN AND FOR _____ COUNTY, STATE OF _____

CIVIL DIVISION

_____,   CASE NO.: _____

\<Name of Lender\>

        Plaintiff

vs.

_____,

\<Your Name\>

        Defendant

REQUEST FOR PRODUCTION OF DOCUMENT

Defendant \<your name\> requests Plaintiff, \<name of bank\> produce within thirty (30)

days of the service hereof, at \<your address\>, the original Promissory Note signed by

Defendant on \<date you signed the promissory note\>.

           \<Sign Your Name\>
           \<Print Your Name\>
           \<Print Your Address\>

CERTIFICATE OF SERVICE

I HEREBY CERTIFY that a true and correct copy of the above and foregoing has been

furnished by U.S. Mail to \<name and address of Plaintiff / Bank or Mortgage Company\>, this

_____ day of _____, 20___.

           \<Sign Your Name\>
           \<Print Your Name\>

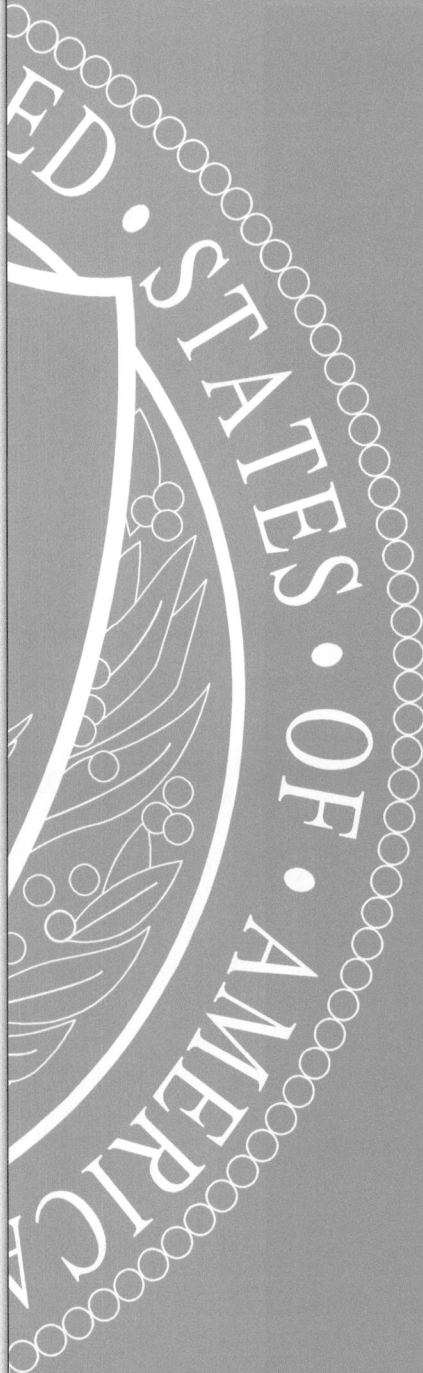

Fair Debt Collection Practices Act

15 U.S.C. §§ 1692-1692p

Last amended July 2010

THE FAIR DEBT COLLECTION PRACTICES ACT
As amended by Pub. L. 111-203, title X, 124 Stat. 2092 (2010)

As a public service, the staff of the Federal Trade Commission (FTC) has prepared the following complete text of the Fair Debt Collection Practices Act (FDCPA), 15 U.S.C. §§ 1692-1692p.

Please note that the format of the text differs in minor ways from the U.S. Code and West's U.S. Code Annotated. For example, this version uses FDCPA section numbers in the headings. In addition, the relevant U.S. Code citation is included with each section heading. Although the staff has made every effort to transcribe the statutory material accurately, this compendium is intended as a convenience for the public and not a substitute for the text in the U.S. Code.

TABLE OF CONTENTS

15 USC 1601 note

§ 801. Short Title

This title may be cited as the "Fair Debt Collection Practices Act."

15 USC 1692

§ 802. Congressional findings and declaration of purpose

(a) Abusive practices

There is abundant evidence of the use of abusive, deceptive, and unfair debt collection practices by many debt collectors. Abusive debt collection practices contribute to the number of personal bankruptcies, to marital instability, to the loss of jobs, and to invasions of individual privacy.

(b) Inadequacy of laws

Existing laws and procedures for redressing these injuries are inadequate to protect consumers.

(c) Available non-abusive collection methods

Means other than misrepresentation or other abusive debt collection practices are available for the effective collection of debts.

(d) Interstate commerce

Abusive debt collection practices are carried on to a substantial extent in interstate commerce and through means and instrumentalities of such commerce. Even where abusive debt collection practices are purely intrastate in character, they nevertheless directly affect interstate commerce.

(e) Purposes

It is the purpose of this title to eliminate abusive debt collection practices by debt collectors, to insure that those debt collectors who refrain from using abusive debt collection practices are not competitively disadvantaged, and to promote consistent State action to protect consumers against debt collection abuses.

§ 801   15 USC 1601 note

2

§ 803. Definitions

15 USC 1692a

As used in this title—

(1) The term "Bureau" means the Bureau of Consumer Financial Protection.

(2) The term "communication" means the conveying of information regarding a debt directly or indirectly to any person through any medium.

(3) The term "consumer" means any natural person obligated or allegedly obligated to pay any debt.

(4) The term "creditor" means any person who offers or extends credit creating a debt or to whom a debt is owed, but such term does not include any person to the extent that he receives an assignment or transfer of a debt in default solely for the purpose of facilitating collection of such debt for another.

(5) The term "debt" means any obligation or alleged obligation of a consumer to pay money arising out of a transaction in which the money, property, insurance or services which are the subject of the transaction are primarily for personal, family, or household purposes, whether or not such obligation has been reduced to judgment.

(6) The term "debt collector" means any person who uses any instrumentality of interstate commerce or the mails in any business the principal purpose of which is the collection of any debts, or who regularly collects or attempts to collect, directly or indirectly, debts owed or due or asserted to be owed or due another. Notwithstanding the exclusion provided by clause (F) of the last sentence of this paragraph, the term includes any creditor who, in the process of collecting his own debts, uses any name other than his own which would indicate that a third person is collecting or attempting to collect such debts. For the purpose of section 808(6), such term also includes any person who uses any instrumentality of interstate commerce or the mails in any business the principal purpose of which is the

§ 803   15 USC 1692a

3

enforcement of security interests. The term does not include—

(A) any officer or employee of a creditor while, in the name of the creditor, collecting debts for such creditor;

(B) any person while acting as a debt collector for another person, both of whom are related by common ownership or affiliated by corporate control, if the person acting as a debt collector does so only for persons to whom it is so related or affiliated and if the principal business of such person is not the collection of debts;

(C) any officer or employee of the United States or any State to the extent that collecting or attempting to collect any debt is in the performance of his official duties;

(D) any person while serving or attempting to serve legal process on any other person in connection with the judicial enforcement of any debt;

(E) any nonprofit organization which, at the request of consumers, performs bona fide consumer credit counseling and assists consumers in the liquidation of their debts by receiving payments from such consumers and distributing such amounts to creditors; and

(F) any person collecting or attempting to collect any debt owed or due or asserted to be owed or due another to the extent such activity

   (i) is incidental to a bona fide fiduciary obligation or a bona fide escrow arrangement;

   (ii) concerns a debt which was originated by such person;

   (iii) concerns a debt which was not in default at the time it was obtained by such person; or

   (iv) concerns a debt obtained by such person as a secured party in a commercial credit transaction involving the creditor.

§ 803   15 USC 1692a

4

(7) The term "location information" means a consumer's place of abode and his telephone number at such place, or his place of employment.

(8) The term "State" means any State, territory, or possession of the United States, the District of Columbia, the Commonwealth of Puerto Rico, or any political subdivision of any of the foregoing.

§ 804. Acquisition of location information

Any debt collector communicating with any person other than the consumer for the purpose of acquiring location information about the consumer shall—

15 USC 1692b

(1) identify himself, state that he is confirming or correcting location information concerning the consumer, and, only if expressly requested, identify his employer;

(2) not state that such consumer owes any debt;

(3) not communicate with any such person more than once unless requested to do so by such person or unless the debt collector reasonably believes that the earlier response of such person is erroneous or incomplete and that such person now has correct or complete location information;

(4) not communicate by post card;

(5) not use any language or symbol on any envelope or in the contents of any communication effected by the mails or telegram that indicates that the debt collector is in the debt collection business or that the communication relates to the collection of a debt; and

(6) after the debt collector knows the consumer is represented by an attorney with regard to the subject debt and has knowledge of, or can readily ascertain, such attorney's name and address, not communicate with any person other than that attorney, unless the attorney fails to respond within a reasonable period of time to the communication from the debt collector.

§ 803   15 USC 1692a

5

15 USC 1692c

§ 805. Communication in connection with debt collection

(a) Communication with the consumer generally

Without the prior consent of the consumer given directly to the debt collector or the express permission of a court of competent jurisdiction, a debt collector may not communicate with a consumer in connection with the collection of any debt—

(1) at any unusual time or place or a time or place known or which should be known to be inconvenient to the consumer. In the absence of knowledge of circumstances to the contrary, a debt collector shall assume that the convenient time for communicating with a consumer is after 8 o'clock antimeridian and before 9 o'clock postmeridian, local time at the consumer's location;

(2) if the debt collector knows the consumer is represented by an attorney with respect to such debt and has knowledge of, or can readily ascertain, such attorney's name and address, unless the attorney fails to respond within a reasonable period of time to a communication from the debt collector or unless the attorney consents to direct communication with the consumer; or

(3) at the consumer's place of employment if the debt collector knows or has reason to know that the consumer's employer prohibits the consumer from receiving such communication.

(b) Communication with third parties

Except as provided in section 804, without the prior consent of the consumer given directly to the debt collector, or the express permission of a court of competent jurisdiction, or as reasonably necessary to effectuate a postjudgment judicial remedy, a debt collector may not communicate, in connection with the collection of any debt, with any person other than a consumer, his attorney, a consumer reporting agency if otherwise permitted by law, the creditor, the attorney of the creditor, or the attorney of the debt collector.

(c) Ceasing communication

If a consumer notifies a debt collector in writing that the

§ 805   15 USC 1692c

6

consumer refuses to pay a debt or that the consumer wishes the debt collector to cease further communication with the consumer, the debt collector shall not communicate further with the consumer with respect to such debt, except—

(1) to advise the consumer that the debt collector's further efforts are being terminated;

(2) to notify the consumer that the debt collector or creditor may invoke specified remedies which are ordinarily invoked by such debt collector or creditor; or

(3) where applicable, to notify the consumer that the debt collector or creditor intends to invoke a specified remedy.

If such notice from the consumer is made by mail, notification shall be complete upon receipt.

(d) "Consumer" defined

For the purpose of this section, the term "consumer" includes the consumer's spouse, parent (if the consumer is a minor), guardian, executor, or administrator.

§ 806. Harassment or abuse

15 USC 1692d

A debt collector may not engage in any conduct the natural consequence of which is to harass, oppress, or abuse any person in connection with the collection of a debt. Without limiting the general application of the foregoing, the following conduct is a violation of this section:

(1) The use or threat of use of violence or other criminal means to harm the physical person, reputation, or property of any person.

(2) The use of obscene or profane language or language the natural consequence of which is to abuse the hearer or reader.

(3) The publication of a list of consumers who allegedly refuse to pay debts, except to a consumer reporting agency or to persons meeting the requirements of section 603(f) or 604(3)[1] of this Act.

---

1. Section 604(3) has been renumbered as Section 604(a)(3).

§ 805   15 USC 1692c

7

(4) The advertisement for sale of any debt to coerce payment of the debt.

(5) Causing a telephone to ring or engaging any person in telephone conversation repeatedly or continuously with intent to annoy, abuse, or harass any person at the called number.

(6) Except as provided in section 804, the placement of telephone calls without meaningful disclosure of the caller's identity.

15 USC 1692e

§ 807. False or misleading representations

A debt collector may not use any false, deceptive, or misleading representation or means in connection with the collection of any debt. Without limiting the general application of the foregoing, the following conduct is a violation of this section:

(1) The false representation or implication that the debt collector is vouched for, bonded by, or affiliated with the United States or any State, including the use of any badge, uniform, or facsimile thereof.

(2) The false representation of—

(A) the character, amount, or legal status of any debt; or

(B) any services rendered or compensation which may be lawfully received by any debt collector for the collection of a debt.

(3) The false representation or implication that any individual is an attorney or that any communication is from an attorney.

(4) The representation or implication that nonpayment of any debt will result in the arrest or imprisonment of any person or the seizure, garnishment, attachment, or sale of any property or wages of any person unless such action is lawful and the debt collector or creditor intends to take such action.

(5) The threat to take any action that cannot legally be taken or that is not intended to be taken.

§ 806   15 USC 1692d

8

(6) The false representation or implication that a sale, referral, or other transfer of any interest in a debt shall cause the consumer to—

(A) lose any claim or defense to payment of the debt; or

(B) become subject to any practice prohibited by this title.

(7) The false representation or implication that the consumer committed any crime or other conduct in order to disgrace the consumer.

(8) Communicating or threatening to communicate to any person credit information which is known or which should be known to be false, including the failure to communicate that a disputed debt is disputed.

(9) The use or distribution of any written communication which simulates or is falsely represented to be a document authorized, issued, or approved by any court, official, or agency of the United States or any State, or which creates a false impression as to its source, authorization, or approval.

(10) The use of any false representation or deceptive means to collect or attempt to collect any debt or to obtain information concerning a consumer.

(11) The failure to disclose in the initial written communication with the consumer and, in addition, if the initial communication with the consumer is oral, in that initial oral communication, that the debt collector is attempting to collect a debt and that any information obtained will be used for that purpose, and the failure to disclose in subsequent communications that the communication is from a debt collector, except that this paragraph shall not apply to a formal pleading made in connection with a legal action.

(12) The false representation or implication that accounts have been turned over to innocent purchasers for value.

(13) The false representation or implication that documents are legal process.

§ 807   15 USC 1692e

9

(14) The use of any business, company, or organization name other than the true name of the debt collector's business, company, or organization.

(15) The false representation or implication that documents are not legal process forms or do not require action by the consumer.

(16) The false representation or implication that a debt collector operates or is employed by a consumer reporting agency as defined by section 603(f) of this Act.

15 USC 1692f

§ 808. Unfair practices

A debt collector may not use unfair or unconscionable means to collect or attempt to collect any debt. Without limiting the general application of the foregoing, the following conduct is a violation of this section:

(1) The collection of any amount (including any interest, fee, charge, or expense incidental to the principal obligation) unless such amount is expressly authorized by the agreement creating the debt or permitted by law.

(2) The acceptance by a debt collector from any person of a check or other payment instrument postdated by more than five days unless such person is notified in writing of the debt collector's intent to deposit such check or instrument not more than ten nor less than three business days prior to such deposit.

(3) The solicitation by a debt collector of any postdated check or other postdated payment instrument for the purpose of threatening or instituting criminal prosecution.

(4) Depositing or threatening to deposit any postdated check or other postdated payment instrument prior to the date on such check or instrument.

(5) Causing charges to be made to any person for communications by concealment of the true propose of the communication. Such charges include, but are not limited to, collect telephone calls and telegram fees.

(6) Taking or threatening to take any nonjudicial action to effect dispossession or disablement of property if—

§ 807   15 USC 1692e

10

(A) there is no present right to possession of the property claimed as collateral through an enforceable security interest;

(B) there is no present intention to take possession of the property; or

(C) the property is exempt by law from such dispossession or disablement.

(7) Communicating with a consumer regarding a debt by post card.

(8) Using any language or symbol, other than the debt collector's address, on any envelope when communicating with a consumer by use of the mails or by telegram, except that a debt collector may use his business name if such name does not indicate that he is in the debt collection business.

§ 809. Validation of debts

15 USC 1692g

(a) Notice of debt; contents

Within five days after the initial communication with a consumer in connection with the collection of any debt, a debt collector shall, unless the following information is contained in the initial communication or the consumer has paid the debt, send the consumer a written notice containing—

(1) the amount of the debt;

(2) the name of the creditor to whom the debt is owed;

(3) a statement that unless the consumer, within thirty days after receipt of the notice, disputes the validity of the debt, or any portion thereof, the debt will be assumed to be valid by the debt collector;

(4) a statement that if the consumer notifies the debt collector in writing within the thirty-day period that the debt, or any portion thereof, is disputed, the debt collector will obtain verification of the debt or a copy of a judgment against the consumer and a copy of such verification or judgment will be mailed to the consumer by the debt collector; and

§ 808   15 USC 1692f

11

(5) a statement that, upon the consumer's written request within the thirty-day period, the debt collector will provide the consumer with the name and address of the original creditor, if different from the current creditor.

(b) Disputed debts

If the consumer notifies the debt collector in writing within the thirty-day period described in subsection (a) that the debt, or any portion thereof, is disputed, or that the consumer requests the name and address of the original creditor, the debt collector shall cease collection of the debt, or any disputed portion thereof, until the debt collector obtains verification of the debt or any copy of a judgment, or the name and address of the original creditor, and a copy of such verification or judgment, or name and address of the original creditor, is mailed to the consumer by the debt collector. Collection activities and communications that do not otherwise violate this title may continue during the 30-day period referred to in subsection (a) unless the consumer has notified the debt collector in writing that the debt, or any portion of the debt, is disputed or that the consumer requests the name and address of the original creditor. Any collection activities and communication during the 30-day period may not overshadow or be inconsistent with the disclosure of the consumer's right to dispute the debt or request the name and address of the original creditor.

(c) Admission of liability

The failure of a consumer to dispute the validity of a debt under this section may not be construed by any court as an admission of liability by the consumer.

(d) Legal pleadings

A communication in the form of a formal pleading in a civil action shall not be treated as an initial communication for purposes of subsection (a).

(e) Notice provisions

The sending or delivery of any form or notice which does not relate to the collection of a debt and is expressly

§ 809   15 USC 1692g required by the Internal Revenue Code of 1986, title V of Gramm-Leach-Bliley Act, or any provision of Federal or State law relating to notice of data security breach or privacy, or any regulation prescribed under any such provision of law, shall not be treated as an initial communication in connection with debt collection for purposes of this section.

§ 810. Multiple debts

15 USC 1692h

If any consumer owes multiple debts and makes any single payment to any debt collector with respect to such debts, such debt collector may not apply such payment to any debt which is disputed by the consumer and, where applicable, shall apply such payment in accordance with the consumer's directions.

§ 811. Legal actions by debt collectors

15 USC 1692i

(a) Venue

Any debt collector who brings any legal action on a debt against any consumer shall—

(1) in the case of an action to enforce an interest in real property securing the consumer's obligation, bring such action only in a judicial district or similar legal entity in which such real property is located; or

(2) in the case of an action not described in paragraph (1), bring such action only in the judicial district or similar legal entity—

(A) in which such consumer signed the contract sued upon; or

(B) in which such consumer resides at the commencement of the action.

(b) Authorization of actions

Nothing in this title shall be construed to authorize the bringing of legal actions by debt collectors.

§ 809

15 USC 1692g

13

15 USC 1692j

§ 812. Furnishing certain deceptive forms

(a) It is unlawful to design, compile, and furnish any form knowing that such form would be used to create the false belief in a consumer that a person other than the creditor of such consumer is participating in the collection of or in an attempt to collect a debt such consumer allegedly owes such creditor, when in fact such person is not so participating.

(b) Any person who violates this section shall be liable to the same extent and in the same manner as a debt collector is liable under section 813 for failure to comply with a provision of this title.

15 USC 1692k

§ 813. Civil liability

(a) Amount of damages

Except as otherwise provided by this section, any debt collector who fails to comply with any provision of this title with respect to any person is liable to such person in an amount equal to the sum of—

(1) any actual damage sustained by such person as a result of such failure;

(2) (A) in the case of any action by an individual, such additional damages as the court may allow, but not exceeding $1,000; or

(B) in the case of a class action,

    (i)   such amount for each named plaintiff as could be recovered under subparagraph (A), and

    (ii) such amount as the court may allow for all other class members, without regard to a minimum individual recovery, not to exceed the lesser of $500,000 or 1 per centum of the net worth of the debt collector; and

(3) in the case of any successful action to enforce the foregoing liability, the costs of the action, together with a reasonable attorney's fee as determined by the court. On a finding by the court that an action under this sec-

tion was brought in bad faith and for the purpose of harassment, the court may award to the defendant attorney's fees reasonable in relation to the work expended and costs.

(b) Factors considered by court

In determining the amount of liability in any action under subsection (a), the court shall consider, among other relevant factors—

(1) in any individual action under subsection (a)(2)(A), the frequency and persistence of noncompliance by the debt collector, the nature of such noncompliance, and the extent to which such noncompliance was intentional; or

(2) in any class action under subsection (a)(2)(B), the frequency and persistence of noncompliance by the debt collector, the nature of such noncompliance, the resources of the debt collector, the number of persons adversely affected, and the extent to which the debt collector's noncompliance was intentional.

(c) Intent

A debt collector may not be held liable in any action brought under this title if the debt collector shows by a preponderance of evidence that the violation was not intentional and resulted from a bona fide error notwithstanding the maintenance of procedures reasonably adapted to avoid any such error.

(d) Jurisdiction

An action to enforce any liability created by this title may be brought in any appropriate United States district court without regard to the amount in controversy, or in any other court of competent jurisdiction, within one year from the date on which the violation occurs.

(e) Advisory opinions of Bureau

No provision of this section imposing any liability shall apply to any act done or omitted in good faith in conformity with any advisory opinion of the Bureau, notwith-

§ 813   15 USC 1692k

15

standing that after such act or omission has occurred, such opinion is amended, rescinded, or determined by judicial or other authority to be invalid for any reason.

15 USC 1692*l*

§ 814. Administrative enforcement

(a) Federal Trade Commission

The Federal Trade Commission shall be authorized to enforce compliance with this subchapter, except to the extent that enforcement of the requirements imposed under this subchapter is specifically committed to another Government agency under any of paragraphs (1) through (5) of subsection (b), subject to subtitle B of the Consumer Financial Protection Act of 2010 [12 U.S.C. 5511 et seq.]. For purpose of the exercise by the Federal Trade Commission of its functions and powers under the Federal Trade Commission Act (15 U.S.C. 41 et seq.), a violation of this subchapter shall be deemed an unfair or deceptive act or practice in violation of that Act. All of the functions and powers of the Federal Trade Commission under the Federal Trade Commission Act are available to the Federal Trade Commission to enforce compliance by any person with this subchapter, irrespective of whether that person is engaged in commerce or meets any other jurisdictional tests under the Federal Trade Commission Act, including the power to enforce the provisions of this subchapter, in the same manner as if the violation had been a violation of a Federal Trade Commission trade regulation rule.

(b) Applicable provisions of law

Subject to subtitle B of the Consumer Financial Protection Act of 2010, compliance with any requirements imposed under this subchapter shall be enforced under—

(1) section 8 of the Federal Deposit Insurance Act [12 U.S.C. 1818], by the appropriate Federal banking agency, as defined in section 3(q) of the Federal Deposit Insurance Act (12 U.S.C. 1813(q)), with respect to—

§ 813   15 USC 1692k

16

(A) national banks, Federal savings associations, and Federal branches and Federal agencies of foreign banks;

(B) member banks of the Federal Reserve System (other than national banks), branches and agencies of foreign banks (other than Federal branches, Federal agencies, and insured State branches of foreign banks), commercial lending companies owned or controlled by foreign banks, and organizations operating under section 25 or 25A of the Federal Reserve Act [12 U.S.C. 601 et seq., 611 et seq.]; and

(C) banks and State savings associations insured by the Federal Deposit Insurance Corporation (other than members of the Federal Reserve System), and insured State branches of foreign banks;

(2) the Federal Credit Union Act [12 U.S.C. 1751 et seq.], by the Administrator of the National Credit Union Administration with respect to any Federal credit union;

(3) subtitle IV of title 49, by the Secretary of Transportation, with respect to all carriers subject to the jurisdiction of the Surface Transportation Board;

(4) part A of subtitle VII of title 49, by the Secretary of Transportation with respect to any air carrier or any foreign air carrier subject to that part;

(5) the Packers and Stockyards Act, 1921 [7 U.S.C. 181 et seq.] (except as provided in section 406 of that Act [7 U.S.C. 226, 227]), by the Secretary of Agriculture with respect to any activities subject to that Act; and

(6) subtitle E of the Consumer Financial Protection Act of 2010 [12 U.S.C. 5561 et seq.], by the Bureau, with respect to any person subject to this subchapter.

The terms used in paragraph (1) that are not defined in this subchapter or otherwise defined in section 3(s) of the Federal Deposit Insurance Act (12 U.S.C. 1813(s)) shall have the meaning given to them in section 1(b) of the International Banking Act of 1978 (12 U.S.C. 3101).

§ 814   15 USC 1692*l*

17

(c) Agency powers

For the purpose of the exercise by any agency referred to in subsection (b) of this section of its powers under any Act referred to in that subsection, a violation of any requirement imposed under this subchapter shall be deemed to be a violation of a requirement imposed under that Act. In addition to its powers under any provision of law specifically referred to in subsection (b) of this section, each of the agencies referred to in that subsection may exercise, for the purpose of enforcing compliance with any requirement imposed under this subchapter any other authority conferred on it by law, except as provided in subsection (d) of this section.

(d) Rules and regulations

Except as provided in section 1029(a) of the Consumer Financial Protection Act of 2010 [12 U.S.C. 5519(a)], the Bureau may prescribe rules with respect to the collection of debts by debt collectors, as defined in this subchapter.

15 USC 1692m

§ 815. Reports to Congress by the Bureau; views of other Federal agencies

(a) Not later than one year after the effective date of this title and at one-year intervals thereafter, the Bureau shall make reports to the Congress concerning the administration of its functions under this title, including such recommendations as the Bureau deems necessary or appropriate. In addition, each report of the Bureau shall include its assessment of the extent to which compliance with this title is being achieved and a summary of the enforcement actions taken by the Bureau under section 814 of this title.

(b) In the exercise of its functions under this title, the Bureau may obtain upon request the views of any other Federal agency which exercises enforcement functions under section 814 of this title.

§ 814   15 USC 1692*l*

18

§ 816. Relation to State laws

This title does not annul, alter, or affect, or exempt any person subject to the provisions of this title from complying with the laws of any State with respect to debt collection practices, except to the extent that those laws are inconsistent with any provision of this title, and then only to the extent of the inconsistency. For purposes of this section, a State law is not inconsistent with this title if the protection such law affords any consumer is greater than the protection provided by this title.

§ 817. Exemption for State regulation

The Bureau shall by regulation exempt from the requirements of this title any class of debt collection practices within any State if the Bureau determines that under the law of that State that class of debt collection practices is subject to requirements substantially similar to those imposed by this title, and that there is adequate provision for enforcement.

§ 818. Exception for certain bad check enforcement programs operated by private entities

(a) In general

   (1) Treatment of certain private entities

      Subject to paragraph (2), a private entity shall be excluded from the definition of a debt collector, pursuant to the exception provided in section 803(6), with respect to the operation by the entity of a program described in paragraph (2)(A) under a contract described in paragraph (2)(B).

   (2) Conditions of applicability

      Paragraph (1) shall apply if—

      (A) a State or district attorney establishes, within the jurisdiction of such State or district attorney and with respect to alleged bad check violations that do not involve a check described in subsection (b), a pretrial diversion program for alleged bad check offenders who agree to participate voluntarily in such program to avoid criminal prosecution;

(B) a private entity, that is subject to an administrative support services contract with a State or district attorney and operates under the direction, supervision, and control of such State or district attorney, operates the pretrial diversion program described in subparagraph (A); and

(C) in the course of performing duties delegated to it by a State or district attorney under the contract, the private entity referred to in subparagraph (B)—

  (i) complies with the penal laws of the State;

  (ii) conforms with the terms of the contract and directives of the State or district attorney;

  (iii) does not exercise independent prosecutorial discretion;

  (iv) contacts any alleged offender referred to in subparagraph (A) for purposes of participating in a program referred to in such paragraph—

    (I) only as a result of any determination by the State or district attorney that probable cause of a bad check violation under State penal law exists, and that contact with the alleged offender for purposes of participation in the program is appropriate; and

    (II) the alleged offender has failed to pay the bad check after demand for payment, pursuant to State law, is made for payment of the check amount;

  (v) includes as part of an initial written communication with an alleged offender a clear and conspicuous statement that—

    (I) the alleged offender may dispute the validity of any alleged bad check violation;

    (II) where the alleged offender knows, or has reasonable cause to believe, that the alleged bad check violation is the result of theft or forgery of the check, identity theft,

§ 818   15 USC 1692p

20

or other fraud that is not the result of the conduct of the alleged offender, the alleged offender may file a crime report with the appropriate law enforcement agency; and

(III) if the alleged offender notifies the private entity or the district attorney in writing, not later than 30 days after being contacted for the first time pursuant to clause (iv), that there is a dispute pursuant to this subsection, before further restitution efforts are pursued, the district attorney or an employee of the district attorney authorized to make such a determination makes a determination that there is probable cause to believe that a crime has been committed; and

(vi) charges only fees in connection with services under the contract that have been authorized by the contract with the State or district attorney.

(b) Certain checks excluded

A check is described in this subsection if the check involves, or is subsequently found to involve—

(1) a postdated check presented in connection with a payday loan, or other similar transaction, where the payee of the check knew that the issuer had insufficient funds at the time the check was made, drawn, or delivered;

(2) a stop payment order where the issuer acted in good faith and with reasonable cause in stopping payment on the check;

(3) a check dishonored because of an adjustment to the issuer's account by the financial institution holding such account without providing notice to the person at the time the check was made, drawn, or delivered;

(4) a check for partial payment of a debt where the payee had previously accepted partial payment for such debt;

(5) a check issued by a person who was not competent, or was not of legal age, to enter into a legal contractual

§ 818   15 USC 1692p

21

obligation at the time the check was made, drawn, or delivered; or

(6) a check issued to pay an obligation arising from a transaction that was illegal in the jurisdiction of the State or district attorney at the time the check was made, drawn, or delivered.

(c) Definitions

For purposes of this section, the following definitions shall apply:

(1) State or district attorney

The term "State or district attorney" means the chief elected or appointed prosecuting attorney in a district, county (as defined in section 2 of title 1, United States Code), municipality, or comparable jurisdiction, including State attorneys general who act as chief elected or appointed prosecuting attorneys in a district, county (as so defined), municipality or comparable jurisdiction, who may be referred to by a variety of titles such as district attorneys, prosecuting attorneys, commonwealth's attorneys, solicitors, county attorneys, and state's attorneys, and who are responsible for the prosecution of State crimes and violations of jurisdiction-specific local ordinances.

(2) Check

The term "check" has the same meaning as in section 3(6) of the Check Clearing for the 21st Century Act.

(3) Bad check violation

The term "bad check violation" means a violation of the applicable State criminal law relating to the writing of dishonored checks.

15 USC 1692 note

§ 819. Effective date

This title takes effect upon the expiration of six months after the date of its enactment, but section 809 shall apply only with respect to debts for which the initial attempt to collect occurs after such effective date.

§ 818   15 USC 1692p

LEGISLATIVE HISTORY

House Report: No. 95-131 (Comm. on Banking, Finance, and Urban Affairs)

Senate Report: No. 95-382 (Comm. on Banking, Housing and Urban Affairs)

Congressional Record, Vol. 123 (1977)

> April 4, House considered and passed H.R. 5294.

> Aug. 5, Senate considered and passed amended version of H.R. 5294.

> Sept. 8, House considered and passed Senate version.

Enactment: Public Law 95-109 (September 20, 1977)

Amendments: Public Law Nos.

> 99-361 (July 9, 1986)

> 101-73 (August 9, 1989)

> 102-242 (December 19, 1991)

> 102-550 (October 28, 1992)

> 104-88 (December 29, 1995)

> 104-208 (September 30, 1996)

> 109-351 (October 13, 2006)

> 111-203 (July 21, 2010)

Printed May 2013

23